MW01611804

EMPOWERMENT

TAKES MORE THAN A MINUTE

KEN BLANCHARD
CO-AUTHOR "THE ONE MINUTE MANAGER"

JOHN P. CARLOS AND ALAN RANDOLPH

Publisher's Cataloging in Publication

Blanchard, Kenneth H.

   Empowerment takes more than a minute/ Ken Blanchard, John P. Carlos, Alan Randolph

   p. cm.

   ISBN: 1:56912-088-9

   1. Management 2. Business I. Carlos, John P. II. Randolph, W. Alan. III. Title.

HD31.B53 1995   658

                    QB194-21301

Printed in the United States of America

Dedication

to...

Dorothy Blanchard
Donald L. and Isabella Carlos
Wallace Randolph

who taught us so much about being empowered

F ew changes in business have caught on, yet been so problematic, as the move to create empowered, employee-driven, work environments. Empowerment offers the potential for tapping into a wellspring of underutilized human capacity that must be harnessed if organizations are to survive in today's increasingly complex and dynamic world.

Empowered employees benefit the organization and themselves by being a more integral part of the organizations in which they work and by being able to make a more significant contribution. As a result, they have a greater sense of purpose in their jobs and lives, and their involvement translates directly into improving systems and processes in the workplace and in obtaining continuous improvement in results.

In an empowered organization, employees bring their best ideas and initiatives to the workplace with a sense of excitement, ownership and pride.

In addition, empowered employees act with responsibility, putting the best interests of the organization first.

To create an empowered workplace, management's role in organizations must move from a command-and-control mind set to an emphasis on facilitating a responsibility-oriented and supportive environment in which all employees have the opportunity to do their best. The traditional management model of "the manager in control and employees being controlled" is no longer effective. Instead, managers are finding it necessary to empower workers to perform, so that "more gets done with less."

Shifting to an empowerment philosophy calls for changes in most aspects of an organization. Both managers and employees must first learn not to be bureaucratic and second, to be empowered. The problem is that many managers do not understand that empowerment involves releasing the power people already have, nor do they understand how to navigate the journey to empowerment. *Empowerment Takes More Than a Minute* shows management how to take this journey that is filled with paradox and challenge.

Over the last eight years or so, we have had the opportunity to work on an extended basis with a wide variety of companies that were trying, in one way or another, to create empowered workplaces.

These companies have taught us a great deal about what empowerment is and how to create it. They haven't always known the answers to the questions raised by empowerment and neither have we—quite the contrary. Rather, it has been through missteps that we have learned the three keys to empowerment that are presented in this book.

The journey to empowerment is a long and challenging process that is not for the weak in spirit. For those of you who undertake this journey, we urge you to stay the course. We know that this journey can be made easier if you will start with, and stick to, the three keys of empowerment explained in *Empowerment Takes More Than a Minute*. Good luck on your journey.

Ken Blanchard   *John Carlos*   *Alan Randolph*

The rain beat down steadily. Occasionally the wind threw great splashes against the executive office windows. Inside sat the president and CEO, Laura Day, who had just taken over the company's leadership. Her job was to realign the company with the requirements of today's customers and improve its declining performance—get the company back on a growth track. As she gazed out at the downpour, Laura asked herself whether she had bitten off more than she could chew. She remembered that, as a key vice president of a Fortune 500 Company, she'd been waiting for a promotion from within when she received a call from an executive search firm.

"Would you be interested," the caller had asked, "in a position as president and CEO of a midsize, once-successful company? This company is facing fierce competition. It needs somebody to breathe new life into it and lead the way to recapturing market share."

Always one to relish a challenge, Laura had accepted the position. As the new head of the company, she realized that there was plenty to be done and that fast action was necessary.

Her first move had been to set up a task force made up of customers and representatives from several levels of the company. Their job was to identify what it would take for this organization to move into a position of market leadership.

Another sheet of rain blasted the office windows, rousing Laura from her trance. She looked up at a familiar sign on the wall above her desk and smiled. The sign read:

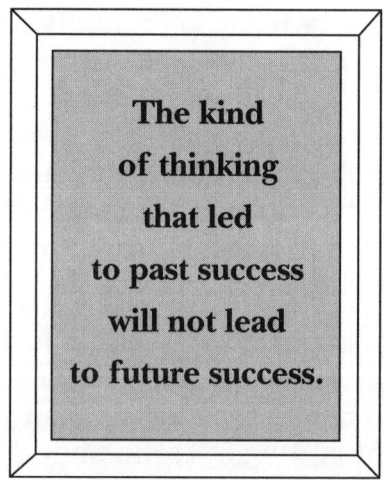

**The kind
of thinking
that led
to past success
will not lead
to future success.**

She recalled posting the sign there after the results of the task-force study had come back. She'd hoped then that the sign would remind her and others of a painfully obvious fact which the study had confirmed—*the first thing that would have to change was management's thinking.*

However, the study had been even more specific than that. In no uncertain terms it had warned that the company would be outstripped by its competition unless all thinking, structure, processes and action conformed to four critical organizational attributes.

The company needed to be

1. Customer-driven

2. Cost-effective

3. Fast and flexible

4. Continually improving

Now, as she had so many times before, Laura mentally reviewed each item on that list.

1. Customer-driven

No one had to convince the new CEO that these days success begins with customers. Just a few years ago, mass-produced products were guaranteed to be consumed, competition was moderate and mostly on a local scale, and customers had few choices.

But change had come with blinding speed. Today's customers were so much more sophisticated, and they were offered so many choices, that any organization not responsive to customers' wants and needs was doomed to be second rate or soon out of business!

2. Cost-effective

The importance of this characteristic didn't surprise Laura, either. Cost increases, together with fierce pricing battles with competitors, had forced companies to shave margins to a fraction of what they had been. This was clearly an era in which you were forced to do far more with far less.

3. Fast and flexible

The third characteristic always brought a sigh from Laura. It pointed in precisely the opposite direction from the company's history. Cumbersome layers of bureaucratic management had slowed decision making at all levels. Changing customer needs had made these levels of hierarchy as deadly as high cholesterol. In the time it took business decisions to move up the hierarchy and back down again, the customer would be long gone. These days buyers no longer cared who Laura Day was—or about anyone else at the top of the organization. It was the frontline people they dealt with who made the difference.

They wanted their contacts in the company, the frontline employees, to be able to make decisions, solve problems and take action *right on the spot.* Clearly, quicker was better.

4. Continually improving

Laura also knew that lifelong learning had to become a norm in her company. She yearned to create an organization that would steadily outdo itself. She wanted all people inside the company to embrace the vision of a corporation that would be better today than it was yesterday, and better tomorrow than today.

Remembering all this, Laura sighed again. As she took on her new challenge she had a big question facing her: *How do you create an organization that is customer driven, cost-effective, fast and flexible, and continually improving?*

It was a big question, all right, but Laura had wasted no time in attempting to answer it. Realizing that the company's structure required retooling, she had appointed an army of task forces throughout the organization. She told them, "Study and recommend how the company can be reorganized in order to be more responsive to customers and at the same time financially sound."

The groups met, did their work and submitted their reports. This time the data spelled it out short and sweet: *We've got to become leaner and meaner, with fewer management layers.*

5

Over the next several months, the company had undergone a significant reduction in work force. Where possible, this was accomplished by natural attrition. In other cases, Laura and her management team made sure that ethical guidelines were followed, so that outplacement would be least disruptive to families.

"That was nine months ago," Laura mused. Today, nothing seemed to be in the way of full-speed-ahead service delivery. The new organizational structure was now a reality. All the information technology systems which the studies had recommended were in place, poised to release the potential of all departments. Throughout the organization, people were now invited to take responsibility and make full use of their skills and abilities.

But as she looked out at the driving rain, Laura wondered, "Where was all that untapped creative energy she should now be seeing channeled into dynamic action? Where was the spirit of responsibility at work?"

The sad truth was that throughout the organization people were acting no differently than they had when the company was a many-layered bureaucracy. No one in this "leaner, meaner" company seemed willing to step up to the plate and take on the challenge. A pall of reluctance hung over the workplace.

Laura looked down at a small stand-up picture frame that stood on her desk. The huge bold letter "**E**" in the center of the picture was surrounded by cartoons of men and women in various company roles going about their business. Their faces were lit with smiles, and their chests were puffed out. Obviously they were feeling proud and in charge of things. That capital "**E**," thought Laura, stood for one word that had captured the concept she was after in all the changes. The word was *empowerment.*

This word had become commonplace in the management journals she read. It had shown up again and again in task-force recommendations. Office memos, mission statements and departmental newsletters blazoned the new value—that everyone throughout the organization should feel *empowered* to carry out the charge of making the company a leader in the new century. Remembering all the people who had approached her with requests to let them become more involved in day-to-day decision making, Laura thought the shift to empowerment would be instantaneous. Unfortunately, that was far from the case.

As Laura took the pulse of the company—meeting with employee groups, visiting the shop floor, asking questions of the front line—she had yet to see people *acting* empowered. In fact, they went about their business just as they had before, when the company was dominated by its deadly bureaucratic mind set.

Everywhere Laura looked, employees' faces were masks of denial. To them, she sensed, empowerment was merely a word—the "E-word." It was driving her crazy! She often thought of the old maxim, "The more things change, the more they stay the same."

"Maybe," she said to herself, "empowerment *is* just another buzzword. Maybe we don't know what empowerment is or how to create an empowered organization."

These were disturbing thoughts for a bright, energetic, corporate leader. Such thoughts could lead her downward into defeat and discouragement. Laura felt a welter of emotions.

Laura's eyes opened wide and her face brightened. Quickly she sat up, opened a drawer in her desk and drew out a small notebook. She turned to a number, reached for the phone, and began to dial. "I need help with this!" she said aloud as she listened anxiously to the ringing at the other end.

Laura had first heard of Bob FitzWilliam when articles in local papers and national business magazines began raving about his turnaround of a textile manufacturing and distribution company that had been caught napping by the advent of the new information economy. He was considered to have an incredibly motivated staff who acted as if they owned the company. A reporter who'd done a series on FitzWilliam had given him the name of "the Empowering Manager," and it had stuck.

Laura had thought several times of calling on the Empowering Manager, but had always procrastinated. They had been introduced once at a civic event, but Laura didn't think he would remember her.

What had come across during their brief meeting was that the Empowering Manager was a no-nonsense kind of leader who tended to be abrupt with people. She had also heard that he answered his own phone. After two rings, she was greeted by a loud "Hello!" There was little doubt that she had the Empowering Manager on the line.

Right away Laura explained who she was and that she was seeking some advice. "We've streamlined our company so people can take more initiative and respond to customers more quickly. But people are still sending decisions back up the hierarchical ladder.

I've talked a lot about empowerment, and I can't understand why..."

"What's your problem?" interrupted the Empowering Manager.

Laura gulped and thought for a moment. Then she said simply, "People won't run with the ball."

"Let me ask you something," said the Empowering Manager. "Have you ever arrived at a store one minute after closing time, only to find out they've locked the door? You needed something badly, and you saw people inside, so you knocked on the door—and nobody even looked up."

"That happened to me just last week!" Laura exclaimed.

"Whose fault do you think it was? Who were you blaming as you drove away?"

"Why, the employees, of course," she answered. "The manager probably wasn't even there. But the workers were clock-watchers. They weren't thinking about me—the customer. They just wanted to get the heck out of there."

"Wrong!" chimed the Empowering Manager.

"Wrong?" repeated Laura in a small voice.

"Of course the employees were anxious to leave. But you're wrong about who's to blame. The fault is the owner's. Whoever the owner is, he or she's done nothing to make the people who work there feel like they "own" the operation. Otherwise, they would have opened the door."

Laura thought that one over in silence.

"Let me ask you another question," the Empowering Manager went on. "If people really had the choice, do you think they'd choose to be magnificent or ordinary at work?"

"Magnificent."

"Oh, come on! Do you really believe that? Or are you just saying it because you think you should believe it?"

"Why do you ask that?" Laura inquired.

"Because I don't have a lot of time here. I need to know about your real, honest-to-goodness, core beliefs. If you don't have a basic faith in people, it's already time for us to hang up."

"Wow," Laura thought, "this guy doesn't mess around."

"I meant what I said," she answered sincerely. "I really think that, given the choice, people would rather do their absolute best at their jobs."

"Well, you're right," replied the Empowering Manager, "and in addition you have to understand that empowerment is *not* giving people power. People already have plenty of power—in the wealth of their knowledge and motivation—to do their jobs magnificently. We define empowerment as letting this power out!"

"But you see," he added in a somewhat mellower tone, "I've learned this the hard way."

"Empowerment has a sense of ownership at its core, and it starts with the belief system of top management. There are a lot of leaders who must get over the notion that people in their organization head off to work every morning saying to themselves, 'How can I get by with doing as little as possible today?'"

"Do you really think leaders have that little trust?" asked Laura.

"Hey, I can only go by their behavior, and by the results they get from their employees, right? It's not that people in organizations are unable to be their best—they're afraid to be their best. Most organizations are set up to catch people doing things wrong rather than right."

Laura thought about that. "You know," she said, "I have to agree with you. I've seen organizations like that." Then she paused, deep in thought, finally saying, "Somehow I think that's part of the problem at my company." Again she paused, then added, "But I'm not a leader like that! I want our company to be a safe place for people, where they're glad to show what they can do!"

"I think you're sincere," said the Empowering Manager, "and I sense that your *real* satisfaction will come when you see your people take charge. I also pick up on your hunger for winning. You obviously don't want to settle for being ordinary. But I know that empowerment is a top-down, values-driven issue. That's why I had to check out your values."

"So I passed, huh?" smiled Laura.

"For now. Can you come by my office at 2 p.m. this coming Tuesday?"

Laura quickly glanced at her calendar and said, "Yes."

As the Empowering Manager began to hang up, he said, "We'll see if we can get you and your company started down the road to the *Land of Empowerment.*"

Shortly before two o'clock the following Tuesday afternoon, Laura Day pulled her car into the parking lot at the Empowering Manager's company and turned off the engine. From the passenger seat she picked up her notebook, opened the cover and looked at the summary statement on the first page. She'd printed it there after her phone conversation with the Empowering Manager.

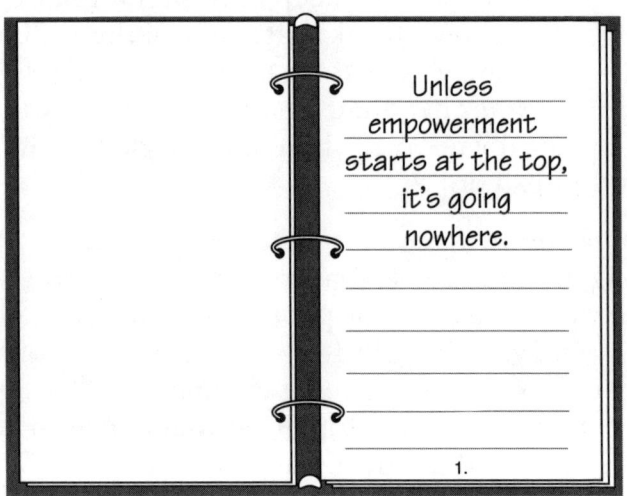

Unless empowerment starts at the top, it's going nowhere.

1.

"You can go right in," smiled the woman at the desk outside the Empowering Manager's office. Laura found Bob FitzWilliam standing by the window looking out. He turned and greeted her with a firm handshake.

"It's a pleasure to see you again," Laura began. "Thank you for giving me some time."

"Don't get too excited until you find out whether or not I can help you. Do you recall what I said as we hung up last week?" the Empowering Manager said seriously.

Laura thought for a minute. "Frankly, no."

"I told you that you were starting on a journey."

"Oh, now I remember," said Laura. "A journey to the Land of Empowerment. I liked that, even though I'm not certain what it means."

"What do you think it means?"

"Well," said Laura, letting her mind roam, "'journey' suggests to me that it might take a while getting there." The Empowering Manager nodded. Encouraged, she went on. "The word 'journey' conjures up tales of adventure, where we follow roads that lead over steep mountains and through dark forests. Unexpected things happen. There are lots of tests along the way."

"Very good," said the Empowering Manager, smiling. "What about the phrase, 'Land of Empowerment'?"

"That's where I get a little foggy. I guess that, first of all, it's a place that's different from the land where I've been living. The ways of the people there are not the same as in the land I'm used to, where I was raised. It's...well...foreign."

"You've done well," said the Empowering Manager with satisfaction. "You've captured the main ideas, the time it takes, and the degree of difficulty. I particularly like your idea of it being foreign—most of us who try to empower others get in our own way because of our traditional thinking."

"Is it really that hard?" asked Laura. The Empowering Manager just stared at her, so she added, "I guess I know the answer. I wouldn't have come here if I'd had an easy time of it. I was hoping you'd just hand me a ready-made formula."

The Empowering Manager smiled, "I'd be doing you a disservice if I gave you a pep talk about empowering people, handed you a set of rules and said, 'Go do it.'"

"As you've already learned, you may want your people to take the initiative, but at first they may not be able to *act* empowered. This shouldn't be surprising. To use your analogy of a foreign land, they don't yet know the language or the customs of the Land of Empowerment." Laura nodded as she began scribbling in her notebook.

"And neither do you know the language," the Empowering Manager went on. "You and your managers may not yet be ready to deal with an empowered workforce. It means learning a whole new way to manage—managing across and up, not managing down. Remember what I told you on the phone—that empowerment is not giving people power—they already have it!"

As Laura nodded, the Empowering Manager pointed to a large plaque on his wall.

People
already have power
through their
knowledge and motivation.

Empowerment
is letting this power
out!

Laura's solemn look told the Empowering Manager that she was mulling this over.

"Whatever happens, it's going to take time for you to get to the Land of Empowerment, and this journey is going to test you and others in your organization time and time again. You'll be impatient because of the lack of quick results. You'll suffer setbacks. You or your associates will question why you ever started or if where you're headed is worth it. The only thing that will keep you going is a huge amount of faith, belief and trust in the journey."

"Have you ever tried to put into action something you believed deeply in, only to find out later that you'd been going about it all wrong?"

"Quite a few times, I'm afraid," Laura smiled.

"You'll have that same experience with empowerment. I can already see you have a commitment to the value of empowering people. You've come here because what you've tried to do so far to empower people in your organization hasn't worked. The question is, are you willing to let go of what you still think is true about it?"

Laura pondered the question. "I think so," she said, "if I understand what you mean."

"My own experience," said the Empowering Manager, "and that of others, suggests that this journey will be a series of discoveries. One of those discoveries may be that the path you have chosen won't get you there. The energy and intention you've devoted to empowering people may have to be rechanneled."

"And that's what you mean when you say that I have to have trust in the journey itself."

"Exactly," said the Empowering Manager.

"I'm beginning to take this journey more seriously," said Laura. "I see that empowerment is not going to happen suddenly, that I have to hang in there. But how will I know if I'm making any progress along the way?"

"That's tricky, too. In the early stages, wins will be small. However, you should keep an eye out for them and celebrate every one. You see, the nature of success itself has changed. There used to be clear signposts, but in these times of turmoil, managers can no longer count on the traditional benchmarks for success."

"Sounds like it's difficult—but not impossible—to know you're getting there. It's just that you have to find a new way to look for the signs," Laura ventured.

"That's exactly right. And there are other, less obvious payoffs, too, which are significant and long lasting, such as changes in attitude, in yourself and in your associates. If you're open and receptive, even the times when you seem side-tracked will yield important findings."

"Also, right in the midst of all that frustration, you'll learn that you are being changed into an empowering person."

"That rings true," Laura said. "I'm getting the impression that whatever you do to empower people while you're on the journey to the Land of Empowerment goes a long way toward making you empowered as well. It's as if the journey and the destination are one and the same.

The two leaders sat quietly for a moment. Then the Empowering Manager spoke, "So, does getting to the Land of Empowerment sound easy?"

"No," said Laura.

"Do you want to go there?"

"I think so. Do I have any choice?"

Smiling, the Empowering Manger handed a pocket-size laminated card to Laura. On it she read:

Congratulations!

You're beginning
the journey to the
Land of Empowerment.

"Thanks," Laura said. "Where do I start?"

The Empowering Manager pointed in the direction of his office door and said, "You have to start out there, with my colleagues in this organization."

"Your colleagues?" Laura repeated.

The Empowering Manager nodded. "The people I work with in this organization, no matter what position they may occupy, are my colleagues, my associates, my partners. If I create an environment that allows them to make this a great organization, they have the potential every day, through their every action, to make that happen. So they are the real source of the information you seek—not me." With that, the Empowering Manager stood up and ushered Laura out the door.

Laura found herself bewildered, standing outside the office. She walked over to the woman who had shown her in. "I'm Laura Day," she said.

"I know," smiled the woman.

"Are you the Empowering Manager's secretary?"

"Actually, I'm his associate," came the reply. Laura found herself thinking, "How did I know she was going to say that?"

Then the woman added, "My name is Amelia Engel. May I help you?"

"I want to find out about how empowerment works around here. So I guess I'd like to talk to some of your...um...associates."

"We're all involved in making this an empowered organization," replied Amelia, "so anyone here could help you."

"Perhaps I should start at the bottom. That's where empowerment really has to go, isn't it?"

"Not really," smiled Amelia. "Anyone who interacts with our customers is considered to be at the top."

"Okay," laughed Laura. "Then maybe I should start at the top."

"Let me suggest that you talk to Juan Gonzales in our Billing Services department," said Amelia, picking up the phone. "They've made tremendous progress in the last year by delivering quality and providing outstanding service. I'll see if Juan is available."

Laura found her way to the billing response center, where Juan had suggested they meet. She was surprised that it appeared to be a standard operation, with the same kinds of equipment her own company used. The people looked the same, too. But at this point she didn't know what to expect.

A young man approached her, "Hi, I'm Juan Gonzales. You must be the executive Amelia called me about. What can I do for you?"

"I just finished talking with the Empowering Manager and now I need to talk with some associates in your company about empowerment. I must tell you, though, that even though empowering people is my goal, I've become something of a skeptic. I've tried to institute empowerment with my associates, and frankly I haven't seen much change."

"How long have you been at it?" Juan asked.

"Nine months," said Laura.

Juan nodded. "All people have doubts at the beginning. But that shouldn't be surprising. They're being asked to buy into something on faith. Not only have they had no experience with being empowered, in many cases they've been unempowered. Also in the beginning they don't know how the process is going to work. They have no sense of *WIIFM*."

"Excuse me. WIIFM?"

"What's-In-It-For-Me. You can't blame people for being skeptical. Enough flavor-of-the-month programs have come and gone for people to believe that this is just another one of them. That was certainly the attitude here."

"In fact, when the Empowering Manager started telling us that his goal was to build an organization of colleagues where everybody's potential would be used, we thought he'd lost his mind."

"Hmm," Laura mused. "That could explain why people aren't acting empowered in my company. I guess beliefs change slowly."

"It takes time. We didn't believe the Empowering Manager knew what he was talking about. But now, we know he was right," Juan added. "And it's not just that people feel better. We're much more effective and efficient than we were before. We feel better about ourselves, our leaders and our company. We feel a real sense of ownership and empowerment."

"Well, talk is cheap," Laura said, somewhat impatiently. She was frustrated at the obvious satisfaction Juan felt with his department. "How did you get where you are today?" she asked. "*Something* must have happened to release all that energy. It didn't just..."

"Information," interrupted Juan.

"Information?" Laura echoed.

"Yes," said Juan, "Information about how the business is doing—profits, scrap, budgets, market share, productivity, defects, and so on."

Juan took a laminated card out of his shirt pocket and handed it to Laura. The card read:

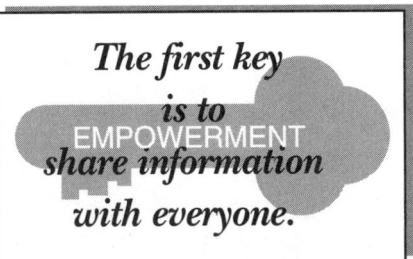

The first key is to share information with everyone.

EMPOWERMENT

"I don't get it," said Laura. "Share information about company performance throughout the organization? That sounds like it could lead to chaos or anarchy. I can't imagine doing that in my company. And further, I think that many others would be very uncomfortable doing it."

"Then you can't create an empowered organization," replied Juan, pausing for emphasis. "I'm going to tell you something. I know you're a CEO, a president and all, and perhaps if I didn't have the Empowering Manager as an example I'd hesitate to say this because of respect for your position. But that's the trouble right there—the *perceived difference in people's positions* that persists from the old hierarchical days. That perceived division between 'superior' and 'subordinate' is no longer very useful in business organizations. In fact, it works directly counter to success. Success today is dependent on team effort."

Juan paused.

Laura nodded, so he went on.

"The most critical place the shift has to occur is inside the leader. Every leader has to fight his or her own battle against habit and tradition in the depths of his or her own heart. Each leader has to make a leap of faith. Those who are unwilling to share information with their people, will never have their people as partners in running the company successfully, and will never have an empowered organization. This act of sharing information is absolutely crucial to empowering an organization. That's why it's the first key."

Laura nodded. "It's certainly going to be a big first step for me."

"Why wouldn't it be?" said Juan. "You happen to be one of those managers who's caught in what we call the Big Left Turn."

"The 'Big Left Turn'? What's that?"

"It's the huge, all-encompassing collapse of traditional boundaries that's taking place in our era, due to the sudden explosion of information. Information is bringing down walls all over the world. It's happening in all our institutions at once and it can be very scary."

"I suddenly have this vision of an old metal ice tray," Laura mused, "that you've just filled with water. All the little square compartments of water are separate. Then suddenly someone reaches in and takes away the divider..."

"...and all the water flows together into one. Excellent analogy," said Juan. "This is what's happening, and for leaders like you and me who've been raised in a different tradition, it's difficult to do something like sharing all the information with everybody. It takes courage. But don't wait around for it to feel good to you. Just take a leap of faith and *do it.* It'll feel good later on."

"Just do it," Laura repeated. "Does that mean with privileged information, too?"

"What do you mean by 'privileged information'?" asked Juan.

"Privileged information means guarded information; known to a few; only certain people have it; sensitive," insisted Laura.

"How would you feel if you were one of the people on the 'outside' who were not privy to the privileged information?" asked Juan.

That caught Laura off guard. She hesitated for a moment and then smiled. "I guess I'd have a lot of negative feelings."

"I bet you would," laughed Juan. "Withholding information carries all kinds of messages. It makes people feel: 'I'm not in the know. They don't trust me. They think I'd do bad things with the information if I knew it. They think I'm too dumb to understand it,' and so forth."

"People don't feel trusted?" Laura reiterated.

Juan nodded. "On the other hand, there's no better way to show people that you trust them than to share sensitive information. Before, information about this company had been kept private and unavailable to most of us. When the Empowering Manager began sharing performance information, he sent a very strong signal to everyone that he trusted us, that he wanted us to use our knowledge and talents."

"So you're saying that trust is crucial for an empowered organization."

Juan nodded enthusiastically. "And if people throughout the organization don't feel trusted, effective decision making grinds to a halt. People don't feel empowered and therefore they don't act empowered. You see:

People without information cannot act responsibly.

People with information are almost compelled to act responsibly.

"That does makes a lot of sense," muttered Laura.

"People without information cannot self-monitor or make sound decisions. People with information can."

Laura began thinking about her own organization. She realized that people at her company did not have the information to really understand the business and its performance results. Nor did they operate with a basic sense of trust. "Sharing privileged information, like the Empowering Manager does, could help people be more responsible and could start us on the road to building trust," she determined.

As she was thinking, Laura suddenly got a "blinding flash of the obvious." She scribbled something in her notebook and then looked Juan square in the eye. "I just got an important insight. Information is the currency for responsibility and trust in the Land of Empowerment."

Juan smiled and nodded. "Every leader wants responsible and trustworthy people in the organization. But stop and think. How do you go about developing responsible, trustworthy people? There's only one way."

"You trust them with information," Laura said.

"And that means action, not words or smiles. You've got to show you trust them by sharing all kinds of information—even sensitive information. Have you talked a lot about empowering people in your company?"

"Oh, we sure have—with no results to show for it!"

"The same thing happened to us," said Juan. "When we began talking about empowerment several years ago, that's all it was, just talk. Nobody really believed anything would happen. We all felt it was just the latest fad. One of my associates who has been around the company for many years, said, 'Just wait, this too shall pass.'"

"The Empowering Manager kept going around saying things like, 'You gotta believe that the magic happens where the work force is.' But we didn't know if he and the other managers really meant it. It wasn't until he began to share information with everyone that we really started to believe. The sharing of what had once been confidential information about performance, profits, true market share and such, made us realize that this was a safe place for us to think and use our real talents and knowledge."

Laura looked again at the card Juan had given her. "Now I see the real *why* behind this first key. I'd always thought of information sharing as being purely functional—you know, linked to people's functions in the organization. So when you gave me this card I was thinking, 'Why do people need all this information to do their job?' But it was the wrong question. Now I realize they need this information to become responsible and to feel trusted!"

"That's it!" exclaimed Juan.

"But what about goals?" sighed Laura. "As you've been explaining that information is the first step to empowering people, I've been wondering about goals. Throughout my career I've always understood that goal setting should be first. If information comes first, where do goals fit in?"

Juan smiled and said, "I was waiting for you to ask that, because everyone does. Goals are still very important. In most organizations goals are established at the top and then handed down. People feel no commitment to them because they haven't been involved in establishing them. I think you can sense how that wouldn't work in an empowered organization. To break down the traditional hierarchical belief that all the 'brains' are at the top of the organization, you have to start building trust first. Once information sharing takes place, and people have begun the journey together toward the Land of Empowerment, then goal setting takes on real meaning."

"So, basically, what you're telling me is wait and see," Laura said.

"That's right," Juan agreed. "Remember, information sharing is only the first step on the journey to the Land of Empowerment. I'd like to tell you more, but I've got to get back to an urgent project right now. Why don't you talk to some other associates about the other keys to empowering people. Janet Wo over in Production is someone I've worked with a lot."

"I happen to know that Janet has a meeting this afternoon, but let me give her a call and see if she'll meet with you tomorrow morning."

Juan set up a meeting for 8 a.m. Laura left the building, with her mind racing with thoughts about what she had learned. When she reached the parking lot she sat in her car for a while, summarizing in her notebook what she had learned.

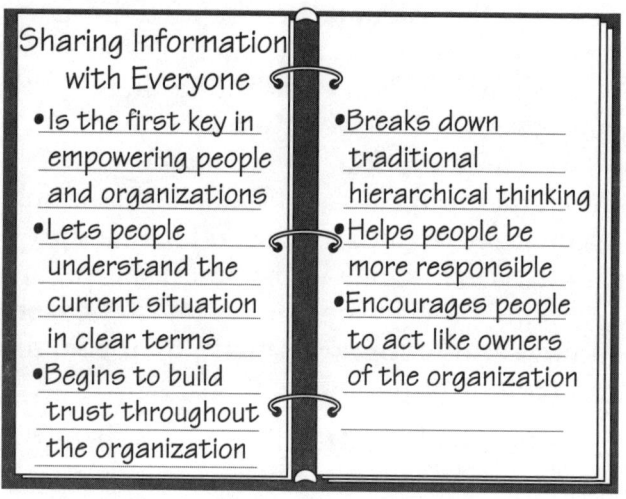

Sharing Information
with Everyone

- Is the first key in empowering people and organizations
- Lets people understand the current situation in clear terms
- Begins to build trust throughout the organization

- Breaks down traditional hierarchical thinking
- Helps people be more responsible
- Encourages people to act like owners of the organization

As she drove home, Laura found that just as the Empowering Manager had said, the new things she had learned clashed with her former beliefs and attitudes. "I wouldn't have thought that information sharing is the first key to empowering people," she thought. "But what are the other keys? And will they be as big a surprise as this one was?"

The next morning Laura was back bright and early at the Empowering Manager's company. As she entered the production area, a woman came up and introduced herself as Janet Wo.

"I understand you've been hanging out with some of my colleagues—the Empowering Manager and Juan Gonzales," said Janet. "This stuff about empowering people can be pretty confusing at first. Remembering how it was for me, I imagine your head is spinning."

"Well, you're right," said Laura. "I'm impressed with how sharing information works to establish trust and help people improve their work processes. But I'm also sure that information in itself is not enough. What comes next?"

"To answer that question, let me ask you to consider things from the viewpoint of management. In order for people to be empowered, do you think they need more structure or less?"

"Why, I'd say less structure. To empower people, you want to free them up, not restrict them with rules."

"Okay," Janet replied in a noncommittal way. "Now, think about where people are 'at' when you embark on the journey to the Land of Empowerment. They've *heard* about empowerment. Most of them probably *want* to be empowered. But what's their total *experience* of what it means to be empowered?"

"Zero."

"That's right."

"I see," Laura mused. "They'd be a little lost. Maybe they would need structure, after all."

"They would, but it's a different kind of structure," said Janet. With that, she handed Laura another laminated card. It read:

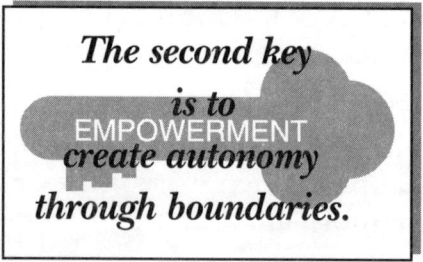

The second key is to create autonomy through boundaries.

"People have to learn new ways of thinking and working together," Janet went on.

"To use an analogy, in the old horse-and-buggy days people used to throw the reins over the horse's neck, and the horse would take them home. That worked because the horse knew the way, but people didn't do that when they were starting out on a journey."

"What you're saying is that with a lack of guidelines, people revert back to their old unempowered habits—they head back home to the familiar," Laura ventured.

Janet nodded. "Yes. Boundaries have the capacity to channel energy in a certain direction. It's like a river—if you were to take away the banks, the river wouldn't be a river anymore. Its momentum and direction would be gone."

"I guess a river without banks would be a very big puddle," said Laura laughing. "I see what you mean. You want people's energy to have direction and impact."

"Also, consider the security there is in boundaries," added Janet. "How would you like to play tennis with just the net—there'd be no lines to define a court. You wouldn't know how to keep score, or what good performance was, or how to improve your game."

Laura thought for a few seconds and then said, "I asked Juan where goal setting fits in and he essentially told me to be patient."

"It would seem to me that goals are an important part of this boundary process."

"Absolutely," said Janet. "But there are other kinds of boundaries besides goal setting." With that Janet walked over to a file cabinet and rummaged through a drawer until she found what she wanted. "Here's a list of the critical areas where we started to create new boundaries," she said. Laura read:

**Boundary Areas
That Create Autonomy**

1. **Purpose**—What business are you in?

2. **Values**—Operational guidelines

3. **Image**—Picture of the future

4. **Goals**—What, when, where and how?

5. **Roles**—Who does what?

6. **Organizational Structure and Systems**

"My goodness," said Laura, "That looks like a lot of structure and boundaries to create."

"It is," answered Janet, "but it need not all be done at the same time. In fact, it can't. It must be done as you need it. In our company it began with top management drafting a compelling vision of our company as an empowered organization."

"A compelling vision," echoed Laura.

"Yes," said Janet. It involves the first three boundary areas. A compelling vision emotionally and intellectually captivates the members of your organization and *crystallizes* their needs, desires, values and beliefs. The way to create a compelling vision is to articulate a picture of the future, an *image*, which clarifies the *purpose* of your organization—what business you are in—and illuminates the guiding *values*."

"Could you give me an example?"

"Sure. Steven Jobs, of Apple Computer, envisioned everyone using a personal computer. The *purpose* of the company was to build and make available affordable information systems—computers. The underlying *value* was to create access to an easy-to-use computer for everyone, not for just a few. The *image* of the end result was a personal computer on every desk and in every household. As his vision became clear, the means to achieve it also became clear, so Jobs developed a method to mass-produce high quality personal computers. A compelling vision creates the 'big picture' for your company."

"Did everyone get involved in clarifying your vision?"

"They sure did," smiled Janet. "Each person in every department translated the vision into roles and goals that had meaning for them personally. We call that 'defining the little picture.'"

"I always think in analogies," said Janet. "In this case, I think of a jigsaw puzzle. The organizational vision is the big picture you end up with when you complete the puzzle. The specific role each person has to play in achieving the vision is like one individual puzzle piece. Each piece of the puzzle has a small picture on it that contributes to the big picture. In terms of our organization, each role has its own little picture."

"When you put it that way, I guess each person's little picture is pretty important," Laura said.

"Absolutely. It's a translation of the big picture into the specific actions that an associate performs. Those actions are directed toward goal accomplishment. For associates to be effective, they must see the big picture *and* their role in achieving that picture."

"Most organizations do goal setting," said Laura. "How is your process different in the context of empowerment?"

"Our goal-setting process focuses energy. Without clear goals people can waste energy."

"Waste energy?" wondered Laura.

"Yes," said Janet. "Have you ever had your employees list ten things they think you hold them accountable for?"

"Why would I do that?" replied Laura. "We tell them what's expected of them, and they all get annual performance reviews."

"You may have just diagnosed one of your biggest problems," said Janet. "Tell me, when people leave their performance review sessions with you, do they act validated or surprised?"

Laura reflected on the last three reviews she'd completed. "Come to think of it, they act surprised. Two of my last three reviews involved disagreements. The people said they didn't know they were responsible for certain areas."

"Sounds like you'd find the *Top 10 Planner* helpful. Since there is often a difference between what people think they're supposed to be doing on a day-to-day basis, and what their manager thinks they should be doing, I recommend that each of them make a list and compare the priority of things on the two lists. Let me give you an example of how this *Top 10 Planner* works."

"A couple who are friends of mine own a convenience store. They were constantly in a quandary as to why things they thought were important weren't getting done around the store. So they asked their assistant to list the ten things she thought she was accountable for. This is the list the assistant produced."

1. Shrink (inventory loss)

2 Cash over or short on the register

3. Stock shelves

4. Clean rest rooms

5. Test gas tanks for water

6. Fresh coffee at all times

7. Clean parking lot

8. Organize back room

9. Stock rotation

10. Ordering

"My friends, the owners, made a list of the ten things they held the assistant accountable for. It looked like this."

1. Sales volume

2. Profit

3. Customer perception

4. Quality of service

5. Cash management

6. Overall store appearance

7. Just-in-time inventory

8. Training employees

9. Protecting assets (maintenance, etc.)

10. Merchandise display

"When they compared lists, the problem became obvious. And as they told me about it they said, 'The fault turned out to be ours as managers. We tell people we'll hold them accountable for end results—i.e., sales, service, etc. But the things we talk to them about day-in and day-out—the things that stick in their minds—are routine tasks. We were sending mixed messages. The *Top 10 Planner* really helped us to see what we were doing and to appreciate the pain we were causing our assistant as a result.'"

"'We'd been telling her things like:

- Shrink is too high.

- Why is the second shift $12 short?

- There are holes in the shelf stock.

- The bathroom is a mess.

- Have you tested the gas tanks for water yet?

- You're out of coffee.

- Who had a party in the parking lot?

- Looks like you cleaned the stockroom with a hand grenade!

- Put the new product in the back.

- Your order is late.'"

"People will never be empowered if they're not sure what their job is. Is it maintenance tasks or is it end results? In this case, the fact that the assistant didn't make the connection between tasks and goals was the owners' fault. Their daily feedback to the assistant fed the wrong goals. They should have been saying things like:

- Let me help you figure out why sales are down.

- What can we do to increase sagging profits?

- Let's find out what our customers think about no coffee and dirty restrooms.

- Our gas customers have an impact on the impulse buying that is an important part of this business. Let's make sure they never get water in their gas tanks.

- If our cash is continually over or short, customers are probably being ripped off.

- First impressions are important. What do you think of the parking lot this morning?

- If the stock room isn't organized, we may have to tell a customer we're out of stock simply because we can't find a product.

- What employee training have you conducted this week?

- What is your schedule for rotating the displays so customers see different products?"

"The difference is what we talk to people about and the way we talk to them," said Laura.

"It's more like being a partner, than being told what to do. I think that if I were the assistant and heard these kinds of messages consistently, I'd have more of a business perspective and feel more ownership."

"We've learned a lot from that story in our company," said Janet. "We've found that, without clear goals that are consistently checked, people can't perform well or be empowered. In fact, highly skilled, creative people will waste a lot of time on less important activities, all the while believing they are doing what is expected of them. In the convenience store example, that might have meant that customers were waiting while someone swept the parking lot."

"I think I've got it," said Laura. "The connection between boundaries and autonomy is getting clearer. I've tried to summarize it on paper in a way that makes sense to me. Please look at this."

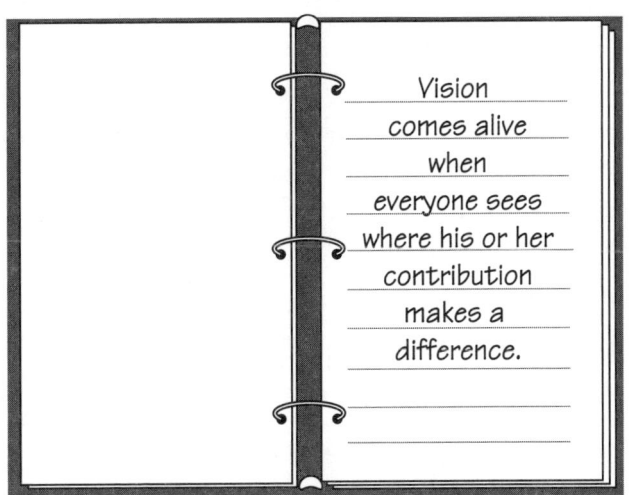

Vision comes alive when everyone sees where his or her contribution makes a difference.

Janet chuckled and said, "Juan told me to watch out for you."

"What do you mean?"

"He said you don't take long to grasp an idea and run with it."

"I guess so. I'm glad to find out where goal setting fits in, but tell me a little more about values," said Laura.

"Values are a key element of a compelling vision," said Janet. "As we began our journey toward the Land of Empowerment, we found we had to clarify our fundamental beliefs and then translate them into commonly agreed-upon values. The former supports the vision, the latter makes it a reality. You see, organizations don't really have values until the associates who work there verify the statements of belief as the way to operate. So the Empowering Manager involved us in a collaborative process of validating our values."

"How did he do that?"

"First he gave us a talk on values. Everybody around here remembers that talk like it was yesterday. People refer to it as the Empowering Manager's I-Have-a-Dream' speech."

"What did he say?"

"*What* he said was pretty important, but the *way* he said it was what really got our attention. It was like he was consulting with us."

"You can't listen to the Empowering Manager long without getting his commitment to certain values. He spelled these out for us, but in such a way that it was obvious that they would work and that they were our values, too. He made us feel important—just like he did when he gave us all that privileged information. Except this time it wasn't, 'I can't believe he's telling us!' It was, 'I can't believe he's asking us!'"

"You mean you felt really involved," smiled Laura.

"Yes. When somebody trusts you like that and asks for your involvement in clarifying values, you say to yourself, 'Why would I work anywhere else?' That speech was only the beginning, though. It was the validation process that followed that eventually got us all aligned with the same values."

"You mean you had an actual method of finding agreement on values?" Laura asked.

"Everyone supported the values that the Empowering Manager articulated. The agreement was more about the rules surrounding those values," answered Janet. "In our work groups we were given a series of directions for creating departmental dialogues. We discussed the values and how they would be acted out in our work."

"How did the meetings go?"

"There were some real surprises at first."

"How so?"

"We didn't know that we had been operating out of differing assumptions until we were involved in the process. As we tried to agree on ways we would operate and treat each other, we kept getting blocked. Once we started discussing the values and listening to each other, as the directions told us to do, our eyes were opened. Defining what was meant by certain key value words became the most important part of the exercise."

"Again and again," continued Janet, "I heard people say, 'I never dreamed you looked at it that way!' One of the guys in my unit said that when we started out we were like a bunch of iron filings, all spread out and pointing in different directions. The validating process was like a magnet passing over us, leaving us all aligned in unison."

"But that must have taken a lot of work time," Laura said.

"As managers, we thought so, too," Janet replied. "We were asking, 'Why are we doing all this stuff, when we need to be filling orders and making money?' But you know what? That process eventually *saved* us time! It was amazing!"

"How do you mean?"

"Ever since the values process, decision making has been much faster and easier. We have a shared set of values to guide us."

"I think I've just made another discovery about my own organization," Laura said.

46

"We've been trying to get one simple statement across to everybody: 'If you see a problem, fix it.' Now I know why it's been so hard getting people to live by that statement."

"Oh?"

"The way we went about it was doubly wrong. First, people didn't choose the rule—it was imposed upon them. Second, we had no process for listening to each other and reaching agreement, like your process for validating values. For all I know, there are as many interpretations of what that statement means as there are people in the company!"

"Without agreement on a rule, you cannot focus energy on your purpose. Values serve as the *driving force* for purpose. All parts of your compelling vision have to be integrated," said Janet.

"Could you tell me how structure and systems fit in?" asked Laura.

"Your vision tells you the right things to do, while your structure and systems, together with defined roles and goals, ensure that things are done right. Let me give you an example," said Janet. "We wanted to coordinate our production activities with our sales districts, so we suggested to them that we needed to improve planning. They were sympathetic, but when it came right down to it they wouldn't make the necessary changes in implementing the planning. Want to know why?"

"Sure."

"Their bonus was calculated on a formula that counted 'planning time' as 'nonproductive.' Planning time reduced their bonus! Once we changed the reward structure, the problem went away."

"So organizational structures and systems that are already in place may hinder the process of empowering people to improve?"

"Right," said Janet. "But remember, these policies were created to support a control-oriented organization, not an empowered one."

Laura thought about that. Then she said, "I can think of policies in my company that would inhibit people from being empowered. One is the requirement of a sign-off for purchases over certain amounts. Another is the demand for formal proposals on any changes that affect more than one department. The list goes on and on."

"Fortunately," assured Janet, "you can deal with each one as you go along. We found that the trust created by shared information made people feel free to express themselves about what was getting in the way of being empowered."

"Right there," said Laura, "is another reason for using the first key—sharing information—to start the process. It creates the basis of trust for the other steps. How did people express themselves, once they felt free to do so?"

"The question we heard most often was, 'Why do we do things this way?' The Empowering Manager encouraged it. Before long, everyone seemed to be examining every rule and policy and system to make sure it contributed to creating an empowered organization. In many cases the existing rules did contribute to empowering people. But a lot of stuff went out the window. The whole organization took on a leaner, more streamlined feel. There were other important questions like: What is my new role?; What do I get to decide?; How will I be held accountable?; What are the new rules?; How do I get some training on my new role?; and others."

"Don't all those questions make for lots of uncertainty?" asked Laura.

"Actually, questions are the *result* of uncertainty," Janet smiled. "Change is always fraught with uncertainty. But in an information-sharing environment, where people operate with trust, uncertainty is something you can handle by communicating, getting agreement and taking action. Such questions are a way of asking for clarification about the new boundaries."

"You know," said Laura, "I get a feeling from people here that you're in it for the long haul."

"Yes, it's a journey. We don't have to do it all at once! I notice you've been writing lots of notes in your book. May I see what you've written?"

"Sure," replied Laura.

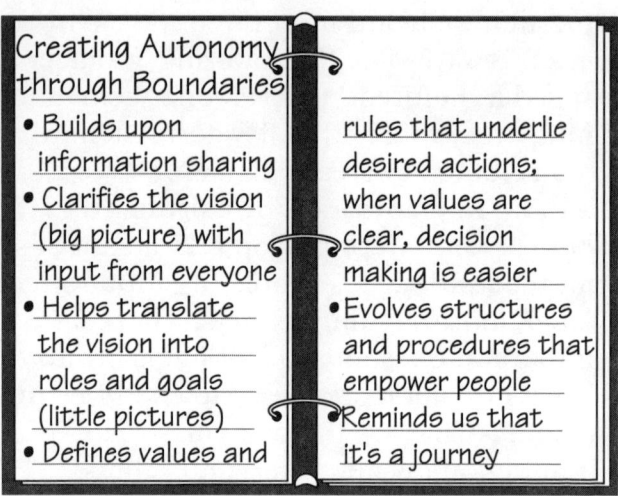

Creating Autonomy through Boundaries
- Builds upon information sharing
- Clarifies the vision (big picture) with input from everyone
- Helps translate the vision into roles and goals (little pictures)
- Defines values and rules that underlie desired actions; when values are clear, decision making is easier
- Evolves structures and procedures that empower people
- Reminds us that it's a journey

"Hey, that's great. You've got it," said Janet.

"It still feels like something is missing," said Laura. "Information sharing, clarifying boundaries—what else?"

"To learn about the third key for the journey to the Land of Empowerment I suggest that you talk to Melvin Borders over in Customer Service."

"Good luck to you on your journey, Laura," Janet said. "I'd like to leave you with something our Empowering Manager said that has always appealed to me: 'Empowerment isn't magic—just some simple ideas and a lot of smart work.'"

As Laura headed over to meet Melvin Borders, she was thinking, "Simple ideas and a lot of smart work. That's what I want for my company."

Laura saw Melvin Borders hurrying toward her as she entered the Customer Service work area. Right away she sensed he was a high-energy person like herself, not much on talk and a pragmatist when it came to ideas.

As Melvin led Laura through the work area, she told him, "I sense you're a busy man, and I want to thank you for taking the time to meet with me. As you may know, I'm here to learn the third key to empowerment."

"No problem," said Melvin, as if dismissing her last statement. "Tell me, did your company recently go through downsizing?"

"Yes, we did," answered Laura. "It's tough being responsible for eliminating jobs."

"I know what you mean. The same thing happened in this company."

"But it was absolutely necessary," Laura quickly added, "to survive and thrive as an organization. In order to be responsive to customers, we needed a company with as few management layers as possible."

Melvin and Laura strolled through groups of industrious people. A couple of associates were talking excitedly together in front of a computer screen. They looked up as Melvin and Laura approached, smiled enthusiastically, and then went back to their task.

"Let me ask you something," Melvin said. "When you finish flattening an organization by eliminating jobs, outsourcing services, and cutting out middle layers of management, what kind of a situation are you left with?"

"Let's see," Laura said thoughtfully. She started counting on the fingers of one hand. "You've got upper management closer to where the action is. You've got supervisors with a wider span of control. And you've got a bunch of people who've been trained to carry out decisions made by others with 'privileged information.'"

"Exactly," said Melvin. "All you're describing is a smaller bureaucracy with fewer layers. Decision making is still moving up the hierarchy. If we want an empowered organization, all that has to change. So the burning question becomes: What's going to take the place of the old hierarchy in terms of decision making?"

"Well," Laura began, "it seems like it would be everyone's responsibility now. But you can't just have an organization of autonomous people acting in isolation from each other. Maybe we need to depend on people working together in teams. People in teams can build off each other's specialized skills and knowledge. Yes, I'd vote for teams."

Melvin nodded. They had been standing in the midst of a bustling stream of people. Melvin led the way over to a couple of chairs at a table on the edge of the work area. Then he handed Laura a laminated card. It read:

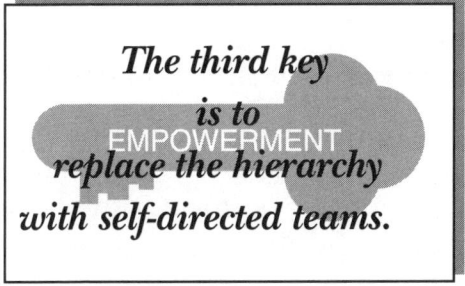

The third key
is to
EMPOWERMENT
replace the hierarchy
with self-directed teams.

"Replace is a pretty harsh word. I don't know how you can do that," exclaimed Laura. "Tell me more."

"Before the change, we'd had participative management and work teams. But they had always been in the context of the traditional hierarchy— mostly one-way communication, with decisions being handed down the line from the top. At best, the teams made recommendations; the managers made the decisions."

"But we realized we were faced with new competition. In our leaner organization we had to stay close to the customer and yet still maintain internal controls that would protect our financial interests. The old hierarchy was too slow and cumbersome to accomplish that. And, as you implied, a team of empowered people is far more powerful than a disconnected set of individuals. So the solution was to get teams to do much of what the management hierarchy had done in the past. Our people had to learn to work in self-directed teams and to make and implement their decisions. Even at the lowest level, people began to grapple with the kinds of responsibilities that had always been left to managers."

"What's a self-directed team?" wondered Laura.

"It's a unique kind of team. It consists of a group of employees with responsibility for an entire process or product. They plan, perform, and manage the work from start to finish."

"Does the team have a manager?"

"There may be a manager on a team," insisted Melvin. "But, if it's a high-performing, self-directed team, you'd never be able to pick that person out. Everyone shares equally in the responsibilities. They might rotate team leadership, but the group would decide how."

"What a shift that must have been!" exclaimed Laura.

"It happened right here," said Melvin as he looked around. "The people you see in this department have become part of high-performing, self-directed teams."

"You say that very proudly," Laura said.

"The mission of our department is an important one," Melvin said. "We're really the sensing arm of the organization, and the problem-solving arm for the customer. We're concerned with anything that goes wrong in the company's effort to serve customers. When an error occurs, we immediately gather all the information about it. Then we feed that information to our production and billing operations so that they understand what's been done wrong and can correct it for the future."

"Sounds like a big responsibility," said Laura.

"It is," agreed Melvin. "On the other hand, it's not too large when viewed as a team effort. No one person has to do it alone. In fact, we who are on customer service teams can't even do it by ourselves. It's the whole organization's responsibility to provide good customer service. Our teams just lead the effort. The point you need to realize is that as teams we are constantly functioning the way only managers did in the past—assessing information from all over the company, analyzing that information, deciding what to do about it, and relaying our decisions to others."

"Hmm," said Laura. "It does appear that people aren't sitting around waiting to be told what to do next. I've been watching your associates as we've been talking. They obviously count on each other, but everybody *acts* like a manager. In a hierarchical operation, people just do their assigned jobs; they don't go out of their way to help someone else. But here, everyone who comes by looks at me and smiles. I can sense their high energy and enthusiasm. They act committed—like it's *their* company."

"Right, but you've got to realize that it hasn't always been that way," said Melvin, smiling. "In the beginning, my associates and I were—well, let's just say we were not immediately committed to this team idea. Many of us thought the idea of being a self-directed team *sounded* good, but we had no experience or understanding of how it would work."

"That's where my associates are in my company," Laura said. "I have all these wonderful ideas from the past two days to bring to them about empowerment and building self-directed teams, but my guess is that they haven't a clue about how to begin to operate in this new way." Laura paused and then said, "It's strange—like wanting something to function freely by itself, but in order for it to do that you have to give it a push!"

"That's a very good way of talking about the paradox you experience in the beginning, before people are empowered."

"You can't just stand around hoping they'll take over. You have to start by giving them what they need at the place where they are. In our case, the managers had to begin with a rather directive style of leadership."

"I've been getting that message," said Laura. "Autonomy begins with the need for boundaries and direction."

"Right," said Melvin. "Guidelines and structure are essential in the beginning of the empowerment journey. People think directive behavior is telling people *how* to do their jobs, but our managers put the emphasis on telling *us* how to *manage* our jobs. It was exciting to suddenly be charged with using all the job knowledge we'd accumulated as a group. Almost everyone had ideas about how we could improve our service and responsiveness to our customers. But we didn't know how to make decisions as a team. We lacked team skills—skills for solving problems, managing meetings, managing the team, and handling conflict."

"So, your managers focused their directive leadership not on telling you what to do, but on developing the skills that were going to enable you to function on your own together."

"Right."

Laura had been summarizing in her notebook again. She showed Melvin what she had written.

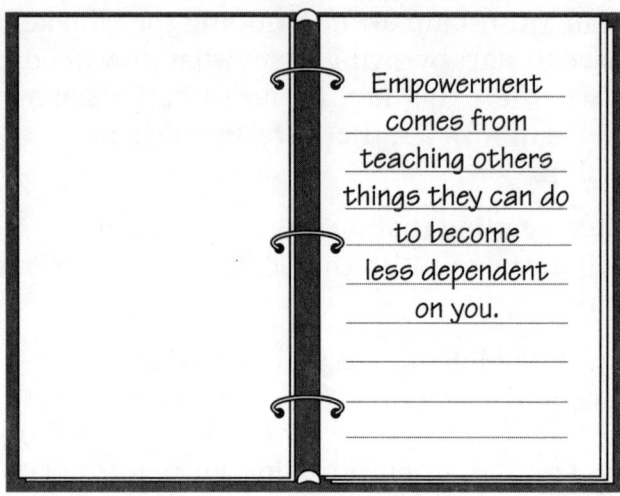

Empowerment
comes from
teaching others
things they can do
to become
less dependent
on you.

"That beautifully captures the idea for the starting point in training teams," responded Melvin. "It was a lesson managers throughout our company had to learn the hard way. In the beginning, they thought the idea was to leave self-directed teams alone. So they abdicated their roles as coaches and then wondered why teams floundered. Everyone on our team was excited at first. But that lasted only for about a week. Then came denial—nobody wanted to admit we were totally confused. We did not want to recognize the widespread dissatisfaction."

"So, what happened?" asked Laura. "Obviously things got straightened out."

"What happened was that the Empowering Manager recognized the state of chaos we were in. He called us all together to help diagnose the trouble."

"He took the blame for the confusion and never pointed a finger at anyone else. That showed us that management was on our side. In the meeting we realized that we wanted to be empowered but that we lacked many of the necessary skills. Together we concluded that we needed training in how to become a self-directed team. We needed strong leadership to guide and direct us. And we needed careful monitoring of our progress."

"In effect, you were asking managers to direct you," said Laura. "So your managers began with a strong directive style. But for you to become empowered sooner or later they had to stop using that style with you. Remember, you said when you become a high performing self-directed team, you can't tell who's the leader. How did the team get away from the need for the directive leadership?"

"Slowly. Gradually. Almost imperceptibly at first," responded Melvin. "Then faster. We began to hear stories of people and teams acting in empowered ways. Teams began to do things that only managers had done in the past, and do them better. Our managers began to act like facilitators and coaches. Some of them started to be masters at choosing just the right moment to do what we call 'standing there.'"

"What's that?"

"It's actually a critical skill of managing to empower."

"You have to know when to follow the rule:

Don't just
do something—
stand there.

"You mean, knowing when *not* to step in so that somebody else can act?" asked Laura.

"Yes. The managers became adept at gradually transferring more and more responsibilities to the teams. Their fears dissipated as they found that there was still plenty for them to do, especially in the areas of cross-functional coordination and cross training."

"I get the idea there's a delicate balance to this matter of transferring," Laura ventured.

"It's a dance," said Melvin. "Like dancing, though, once you get the hang of it, you trust your intuition. In empowering people and teams, you learn new ways of assessing people. The best part is watching employees become associates. It's a lot of fun to 'lead' them occasionally to just a little bit more responsibility than they think they can handle. Then when it turns out you were right and they do handle it, it's great to see the pride in their faces!"

Laura paused, thought for a moment, and said, "You know, this team thing—correction, this empowered-team thing—is really wonderful isn't it?"

"It's very much like a basketball team or a volleyball team that plays really well together. The team members' skills are somewhat transferable but also somewhat unique. They are given a chance to utilize their abilities and to continue to grow and develop. As individuals, they have the chance to become all that they can be and, at the same time, they're helping the organization become all that it can possibly be."

"It sounds like you've got it," said Melvin.

"I think so," said Laura, "but to make sure, let me share with you the key points that I have been listing about the third key to empowerment:

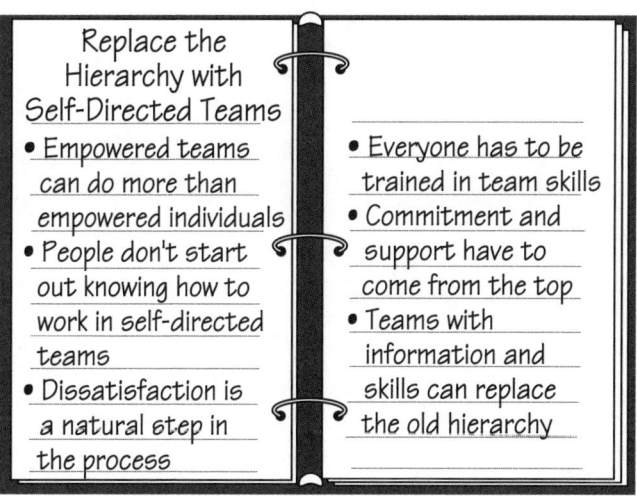

Replace the Hierarchy with Self-Directed Teams
- Empowered teams can do more than empowered individuals
- People don't start out knowing how to work in self-directed teams
- Dissatisfaction is a natural step in the process
- Everyone has to be trained in team skills
- Commitment and support have to come from the top
- Teams with information and skills can replace the old hierarchy

"You're right on the money," smiled Melvin.

"You're a good teacher," insisted Laura.

After Laura thanked Melvin, she headed home. As she drove, Laura could not stop thinking about what she had learned. One burning question that she wished she could answer kept coming to the surface. Finally, it got to her. She picked up the car phone and dialed the Empowering Manager's number.

"I wondered when I would hear from you again," he said.

"May I come by to talk with you right now?" she asked.

"Of course. I'll be waiting."

As Laura walked into the Empowering Manager's office, she found him in his familiar pose staring out the window. As he turned to greet her, she jumped right into her question, "So far, I've learned three keys to empowerment. They sound good, but do they work? Do they make a difference in performance or results?"

The Empowering Manager responded, "Slow down a minute and tell me what you've learned."

"Okay. I've learned that there are three keys to empowerment that are part of a process for releasing the potential that is within people."

Laura showed him her summary notes.

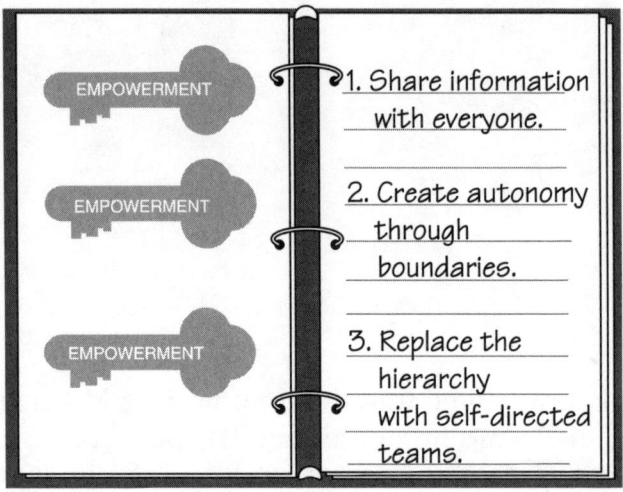

1. Share information with everyone.

2. Create autonomy through boundaries.

3. Replace the hierarchy with self-directed teams.

After the Empowering Manager read her notes, Laura started talking excitedly again, continually referring to her cards and notes. For twenty minutes she talked without letting the Empowering Manager say a word. He sat back in his chair and listened with his hands folded in front of him.

When Laura finished, she was a bit out of breath. She looked at the Empowering Manager and waited for him to say something. Finally he spoke.

"It's evident to me that you understand the steps for creating an empowered organization. You get an 'A' for your solid grasp of the main ideas."

"But can these three keys really lead to empowerment?" Laura asked. "Isn't there more? Do they really improve performance and employee satisfaction?"

"Yes, yes, and yes," replied the Empowering Manager with a smile. "Let me point out a few things regarding performance. This plant has far exceeded even my expectations as we moved to empowerment. Now don't misunderstand; we were the leading plant in our company even before empowerment, but we felt we could do better. And were we ever right!"

"Since we began the empowerment process," he continued, "our quality of production has exceeded 99.99 percent, while our costs have been cut 10 to 15 percent every year."

"On top of that, our people come to work excited every day; they find the increased responsibility very rewarding. And, they continue to come up with new ways to get work done faster, at lower cost, and with higher quality. Our business has been booming and our customers love us."

"That sounds incredible," said Laura. "Could you tell me more about the performance and satisfaction that results from applying each of the three keys to empowerment?"

"Once again I think you'd be better off talking to my colleagues," insisted the Empowering Manager. With that comment, he picked up the phone and called Elizabeth Meadows in Shipping and found that Laura could see her the next morning.

"Elizabeth has some great ideas," he said. "She's right there on the front line and I think you'll find that she's a results-oriented manager who can give you some more insights, particularly about the impact of sharing information and creating boundaries."

"That would be helpful," said Laura. "Do you have any final thoughts before I head off?"

"Two," replied the Empowering Manager. "First of all, as you may already have found, the three keys are simple and easy to understand, but they are difficult to put into everyday action. And, second, the three keys need to be viewed as operating in dynamic interaction with each other. While information sharing is the critical first step, empowering people takes all three, with a constant shifting in emphasis as needed."

Laura nodded, thinking, "*All three in dynamic interaction.*" Then she replied, "Thanks, that helps. I'm looking forward to meeting with Elizabeth Meadows."

Laura arrived early the next morning hoping that Elizabeth could convince her that empowerment worked.

As she reached the shipping area, Laura was greeted by a tall, middle-aged woman. "Hi. I'm Elizabeth Meadows and this is the area my associates and I own."

"What do you mean, you own it?" Laura asked.

"I mean," smiled Elizabeth, "we have all the information we need to make any important decision that has to be made to serve the customer, ensure quality and make a profit for our company."

"Maybe that explains what happened when I was walking down here to meet you this morning," Laura said. "I overheard one of the shipping people telling someone on the phone that the missing items would be replaced at no cost and sent overnight to arrive tomorrow. Frankly, I was amazed. People in shipping don't usually have the authority to make that kind of decision."

Elizabeth, who had been peering over her half-glasses as she listened, said, "Right. But people in shipping *with information* can make that kind of decision and know that it won't hurt the company. In fact, with information they would know just what dividends such excellent customer service will pay in the future. They can weigh the cost versus the benefit of replacing the item at no cost."

"How can they know that?" asked Laura.

Elizabeth gestured to indicate the area around them. "Information!" she said with a smile. For the first time, Laura really took in the graphs and charts that were everywhere on the walls, the computer screens filled with figures, and the people working quickly and with little or no supervision.

"It's impressive all right," Laura said hesitatingly. "I have to admit, though, that I'm still a little skeptical about whether information sharing really works. As a matter of fact, that's why I came back to talk to the Empowering Manager. I needed more reassurance that the three keys to empowerment really work. I am anxious about results."

Elizabeth looked over her glasses into Laura's eyes. Then she asked, "Do you ever write a check to pay for groceries at the supermarket? The cashier verifies your ID and writes the number on the check, right? Then what happens?"

"I usually wait around while the cashier calls the manager or assistant manager to come over and approve the check," answered Laura. "Usually the manager is talking to someone two aisles over as he or she is initialing the check. It doesn't sit right with me."

"Why not?" asked Elizabeth.

"The message it sends is that the store doesn't trust the cashiers and that the only employees there who have brains are the managers. The rest of the people might as well leave their brains at home because maybe they'll need them after work."

"Right," said Elizabeth. "In that process, what do you suppose happens to the cashier's self-esteem?"

"It's eroded."

"Right again. Now, what do you think would happen if the cashiers were given all the detailed information about the impact that bad checks have on the business, and then were given check approval power?"

"Fewer bounced checks?" replied Laura.

"Right! That's what all the research says about places where it's been done. Further, the people have higher self-esteem and can provide more attentive customer service. When you give people information and a chance to act like owners, they'll usually come through," Elizabeth explained.

"Could you give me another example?" asked Laura.

"Sure," said Elizabeth. "A friend of mine owns a restaurant. I was telling her about the power of sharing information with her people. She just wasn't buying it. She didn't think certain information was any of her people's business. To help her move from her 'stuck' position, I had her call together all the folks who work at her restaurant one night at closing time—the hostess, waiters, dish washers, chef, everyone—and had her sit them down at tables in small groups and answer the following question: 'Of every sales dollar that comes into this restaurant, how many cents do you think go to the bottom line as profit that can be returned to me as an owner or reinvested in the business?'"

"What did they say?" wondered Laura.

"The lowest guess from a table was 45 cents and the highest was 75 cents. When my friend told them the correct answer was 8 cents, they were shocked. They thought the restaurant was a money machine. Imagine what that misconception did to their attitude toward things like breakage and food wastage."

"They wouldn't care," said Laura.

"That's for sure," replied Elizabeth. "What really convinced my friend I was right about the power of sharing information was the remark the head chef made: 'You mean if I burn a six-dollar steak that we charge the customer fifteen dollars for, we have to sell at least five steaks to recover the six-dollar loss?'"

"He had it figured out and so did everyone else."

"Interesting," mused Laura. "So they started thinking in business terms. Did it make any difference?"

"Last year my friend declared, 'None of you will get a raise unless you can read our balance sheet and explain what it means.' And for the first time the restaurant showed over a 10 percent profit. When my friend shared 25 percent of that new profit with her staff, they were thrilled and started talking about additional ways they could cut costs and increase profits in the future."

"So you have to *show* people that you trust them by sharing information," commented Laura.

Elizabeth made another sweeping gesture with her arm that took in the department and said, "As I said before, *this place belongs to us.* We own it! Now you can see what our banner means," she said, pointing to a banner on the wall.

Give people the information to act; then look for *magic* to happen!

"Fascinating," said Laura. "How has this worked for you?"

"I've learned that once you share information with everyone and trust starts to develop, you can begin to establish high standards," said Elizabeth. "You can talk about closing the gaps between what's happening today in terms of cost, profits, etc., and what's possible tomorrow, and it makes sense to them."

"Sounds like the TQM idea of continuous improvement," Laura interjected.

"It is," replied Elizabeth. "Continuous improvement only makes sense when people have information and are trusted to use their skills and abilities. That brings me to another important learning. See that?" Elizabeth pointed to a sign.

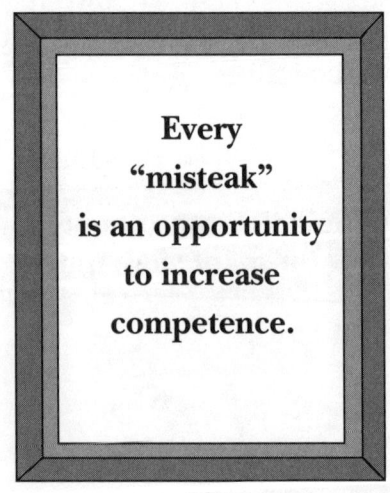

**Every
"misteak"
is an opportunity
to increase
competence.**

Elizabeth said, "The Empowering Manager had those signs posted around the company when we began our journey. Again, everyone thought he was a few bricks short of a full load. The way you're looking at me, I'd say you think so, too."

"It bothers me," Laura said. "I'm a stickler for details, so I feel like correcting the spelling on your sign. More importantly, I don't want mistakes made in our organization. What does making mistakes have to do with improving total quality?"

"Let me ask you something," said Elizabeth. "When a mistake is made in your organization, what's the first question asked—'What can we learn?' or 'Who is to blame?'"

Laura answered, "I've got to admit, most times it's 'Who is to blame?'"

"Sure," agreed Elizabeth. "Now, what is continuous improvement but innovation? And blaming kills the spirit of innovation. People can't innovate while they're busy protecting themselves. On the other hand, permission to take risks, make mistakes, and challenge the way things have been done in the past opens up people's ability to learn and use their talents. That's why the Empowering Manager wanted associates here to see mistakes as okay—to be lighthearted about them—to celebrate them, even."

"Interesting," Laura said. "It reminds me of an article I read abut encouraging innovation."

"I couldn't understand when it mentioned that one company shoots off a cannon every time there's a goof. Now I get it."

"Incidentally," Elizabeth grinned, "if you did go over and correct the spelling on the sign, you'd have some associates here frowning. Since everyone's gotten the message, m-i-s-t-e-a-k has become the official spelling of 'mistake' in our company."

"You mean they're protective of their right to make errors?"

"In a way, I suppose they are. What do you think happens when people are encouraged to make mistakes? Do you think they act more responsibly, or less?"

Laura thought about that. She realized she'd come up against a basic belief about people. "I want to say, they'd act more responsibly. What have you found?"

"They do. That's a significant outcome of empowerment. Shifting the definition of a mistake from something bad or wrong to an opportunity to learn encourages people to think and to monitor their own performance. In other words, it empowers them. And what we're learning, again and again, is that when people are empowered, they do better. What we must do is hold people accountable for nothing but the best, while recognizing that people must make mistakes to continue to improve."

"I think I've just figured out something about this matter of 'misteaks,'" Laura said brightly.

"When people are blamed for mistakes, they become self-protective. In fact, they'll cover up mistakes, in an effort to avoid blame. This limits the information that flows from the mistake, information from which everyone could learn."

"That emphasizes the trust-building element of sharing information," said Elizabeth. "But there are far more practical advantages to the strategy. Want to hear another example?"

Laura nodded. Elizabeth pointed to a chalkboard that had "4 hours" written on it in large letters in the shipping work area.

"Therein lies a tale of continuous improvement based on information," said Elizabeth. "About a year ago we began to look at our performance. We learned that when customers ordered something, it was taking us three to five days before it was shipped. Until we got that information, we never thought much about it. Now that we had it, we wondered, 'Why should it take so long?' We did some checking and learned that in our industry the typical shipping response for an order was about two days. We wanted to do better than twice the industry average! We began to determine how we could improve."

"Now, keep in mind that had we not had the information available to examine, we would not even have been aware of the need for improvement. Also, if some manager had just challenged us to ship orders quicker, we wouldn't have had the commitment."

"I see how that works," said Laura. "The fact that you found it out yourself got you on your own case. And you didn't just know you needed to be better. You decided how much better you needed to be."

"Right. Once we saw the information—especially about how our performance compared to other companies—we knew we had to do something. We made the decision ourselves to change things right here in this department." Laura was noticing the pride Elizabeth took in telling her this story. It was as if she were hearing the owner of the company talk.

"Within one month of becoming aware of the problem," Elizabeth continued excitedly, "we'd cut the shipping response time down to the two-day industry average, but we didn't stop there. We knew we could do better. We wanted to see how far we could take it. We continued to track information on our performance. We began to change the way we responded to orders. Every order was now seen as an opportunity to please a customer. Everyone pulled together as a team. Within another month we had cut our shipping response time down to less than a day. And now, a year later, our typical shipping time is four hours."

"Four hours! Down from three to five days to four hours—that's incredible!" Laura exclaimed.

"Amazing results can come from simply giving people the information with which to work, plus the freedom to operate with that information."

Laura was excited. "I see now that people's full talents can't be used by the organization when they don't feel safe and when they don't have information. When they do feel safe, free to experiment, and apprised of all the information management has, they develop the same feelings as owners. Owners are the ones who feel responsible for everything working right in the company because they have the information to see a more complete picture. Owners don't hold back—they give the success of the company their full attention. When people begin to feel like owners, they begin to act like owners. Now you've got yourself a smarter, more competent organization."

"Right," said Elizabeth, "but let me add one important point: In an empowered organization, position power means very little. Instead we rely on expertise and relationships and on people taking responsibility for their own actions."

"Hey, I like that," said Laura. She had a sudden insight about all the great computer technology her company had at its disposal. Up to now only she and her managers had been using it to share and access sensitive information. The week before a consultant had made a dynamic presentation to her management team which included a demonstration of a new software product called Groupware. Whereas most PC software programs were written for people working alone, Groupware was designed to make it easier for people to work together.

Laura thought, "Wouldn't that make it possible for people throughout the organization to have easy access to almost any information they needed, at the stroke of a few keys?" She made some notes in her notebook, then looked up at Elizabeth.

"I'm wondering," said Laura thoughtfully, "if all people will rise to this challenge. Don't some people just want to get by?"

"Sure," said Elizabeth. "We've found that a small percentage of people simply don't want the extra responsibility and accountability that comes with having more information. But the vast majority do. It's a matter of reactivating their natural desire."

"You think that people would rather be magnificent than ordinary, right?"

"Exactly," said Elizabeth. "It's just that their desire for magnificence is...well...dormant. For years in many organizations you were promoted by doing what you were told. 'Don't rock the boat and you'll get ahead' became a way of life."

"As a result," agreed Laura, "people need to relearn how to take initiative, be responsible and empowered. I think I've got that. Could you talk about how creating autonomy through boundaries makes a difference."

"Of course," agreed Elizabeth. "Why don't we walk over to the cafeteria and get a cup of coffee?"

As they strolled along, Elizabeth began to explain how various kinds of structure take on a new meaning in an empowered organization.

"Once people have the information to understand their current situation, boundaries don't seem like constraints, but rather guidelines for action. Take roles and goals for example. I'm sure Janet Wo talked to you about developing the big picture into little pictures."

"She sure did."

"That's important to us because when it comes to defining roles and goals, our process is a two-way street. Management and informed people throughout the organization work together to develop the big picture, as well as their little pictures. When the vision is clear, everyone knows where their job and their work on individual tasks fits into a bigger picture perspective."

"Can you give me an example?" asked Laura.

"Have you ever returned a new blouse because of a flaw, and been told to take the blouse and the receipt to customer service to get a voucher before you can come back and get a another blouse?"

"Yes," said Laura. "What an inconvenience!"

"Last week," Elizabeth continued, "I went back to a store to exchange a blouse that had a button missing. They didn't have any others in my size. So the salesperson took out a box of buttons, found one that matched and sewed the button on for me right there. While I was waiting I browsed around and ended up buying another blouse. That was a win for both me and the store, wasn't it? But think why that worked so well. I venture to say that, not only was that woman a great salesperson, but the training that she'd received provided boundaries that empowered her to help me."

"You mean, within certain guidelines the clerk had control over what to do," said Laura. "The boundaries provided the playing field and the rules, and on that field the salesperson was free to play her own outstanding game."

Elizabeth smiled and nodded.

"That's certainly a new use of terms like 'boundaries' and 'structure' for me," continued Laura. "In the past, people have become used to working within structure, but the structure's been there to inhibit action, limit thinking and risk taking, and correct mistakes by punishing those responsible."

"You're talking here about new rules and boundaries that encourage responsibility, ownership, and empowerment. How do you get people to make that shift? Won't there be all kinds of problems?"

"We certainly had our share of them," Elizabeth answered. "At first we tried eliminating most rules and structure and using slogans to guide us. But we found that didn't work. People cannot go from a controlled environment to complete freedom and autonomy overnight."

"That sounds like what Melvin Borders was telling me about creating self-directed work teams," said Laura. "Managers have to start with strong, clear leadership and gradually move toward more supporting and delegating styles."

"Yes," Elizabeth affirmed. "There's a paradox here. You need rules and structure so that people are comfortable at first during the changeover. But they are not the old rules and structures that dominated hierarchical life. These new boundaries must demonstrate the values that support your empowerment effort. I made a little desk card that many of us keep around as a reminder of this paradox."

> *New boundaries are there to help everyone learn to act with responsibility and autonomy.*

"Again," said Laura. "I'm feeling the need for an example."

"Good. This example demonstrates our value of 'recovery.' We had shipped some components to a customer, only to find that when the unit was assembled on site, it didn't fit into the space the architect had designed. Our people had met with the architect, visited the building site and followed the specs to the letter, but somehow a mistake had been made. To correct it would cost us $10,000, which amounted to our entire profit for the job."

"That's a sticky one," Laura said with a grimace. "What happened?"

"In the past," Elizabeth continued, "we would have put all our energy into identifying who was to blame—the architect, the customer, or someone in our company. But we have a guideline now that says, 'When a mistake is made, do whatever it takes to recover.' In our training we learned to ask, 'How can we recover so that the customer is happy and so that we get some good learning from this mistake?'"

"That's a great question," Laura exclaimed. "It's got such integrity to it. How did you ever come up with it?"

"It came out of the values and dialogue process we all went through in the beginning. We have a group of rules like this that are basically values questions converted into rules of action."

"If that happened in my company," Laura said,

"some heads would have rolled after we satisfied the customer. So what happened?"

"We assured the customer that the problem would be fixed. Then while we worked with the contractor and architect to modify the space and the unit itself, we had people on the site charting all the changes, their costs, and the other processes of recovery. Later, a task force met to go over the records to see what we could learn from it."

"How did it all turn out?"

"We did more than keep a key customer. The way we handled it resulted in a major referral by that client to another string of companies with whom we've been doing business ever since. And we did get our $10,000 worth of learning out of it. The story of that situation resulted in a renewal of commitment throughout the company of getting things right the first time. The situation assured us that we could 'walk our talk' by following our values-based guidelines instead of indulging in 'poor me' or blaming. It demonstrated the capacity of our structure to encourage people's problem-solving instincts, too."

"The key solution in this situation—modifying both the space and the unit—came from a person who had relatively little to do with the project, but her instincts were right on target. Also, the associates who contributed to the recovery project developed managerial thinking and expertise that has since proved invaluable."

"That's a lot of payoff," thought Laura. "I'm a believer now, that mistakes are opportunities to improve and use our talents, not to find fault."

"You know," said Elizabeth, "it's great having the freedom to operate in this new structure. It's also great to find out that every day you can rise to the standards it implies for responsibility and accountability. There's a sign that hangs in what our team calls our 'powwow room,' that reminds us of this."

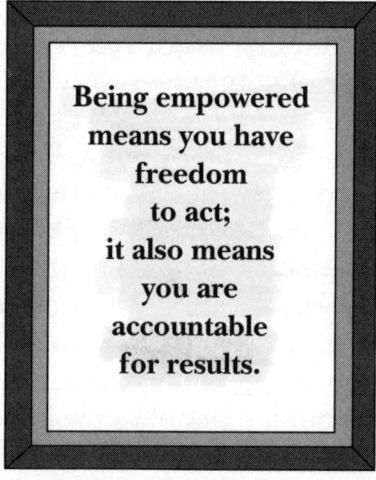

Being empowered means you have freedom to act; it also means you are accountable for results.

"You've certainly added to my understanding about information and boundaries, Elizabeth," said Laura. "And I've already taken up too much of your time today."

"It's been my pleasure," said Elizabeth warmly. "I was just about to suggest you talk to someone in Computer Services about the third key. Billy Abrams over there has a story that will interest you. It's about the nervousness their team had about replacing the hierarchy. I'll walk you over."

"One more point," said Elizabeth as they walked to the Computer Services department, "Nothing is static in the empowerment process. The boundaries we've been talking about will continue to evolve. The evolution will come from all over the organization. People will define goals for themselves and their peers. They'll suggest new roles and improvements. They'll use their teams far more effectively in some cases than you can expect at first. But I'm going to stop there. Telling you about teams is Billy's job."

Laura was surprised to find how young, yet seemingly informed Billy Abrams was.

"So it's my job to show you more about how teams become the hierarchy," Billy told her when they met. "Actually, that's my favorite subject. Probably the fact that I'm team leader this quarter has something to do with it."

"Did top management give you some rules that govern your team's operation?" asked Laura.

"We operate with very few rules from the top," Billy answered. "In fact, we have only four basic rules."

1. Keep customers first and foremost in our actions.

2. Look to the company's financial interests.

3. Be flexible in making quality decisions.

4. Keep others in the company informed.

"But," Laura said, "I've just finished learning from Elizabeth that new rules and boundaries have to be clear to get to empowerment."

"That's right, but they're essential mainly at the beginning of the process," Billy said. "We've come a long way on our journey to get where we are today. We started with a lot of external structure and rules. But now those rules come from within our team. Let me tell you how that happened."

"Good," said Laura.

"More than two years ago when we began our journey," Billy said, "the Empowering Manager told us that his goal was not only to flatten the organizational pyramid, but to turn it upside down for operating decisions."

"What did he mean, turn the pyramid upside down for operating decisions?" asked Laura.

"Suppose you have two phones on your desk, one red and one blue," said Billy. "The red phone is a direct line to the chairman of the board. The blue phone is a direct line to customers. Both phones start ringing at the same time. Which do you answer first?"

Laura paused in reflection and then said, "To be perfectly honest, the red phone."

"Right. And that," said Billy, "is the problem with most organizations. The pyramid is inverted only when it's safe for you to answer the blue phone first. I happen to know that your company has gone through a downsizing like we did. But mere downsizing does little to change the fundamental way that work gets done in a corporation. Without taking some specific steps such as those you've been learning about here, it remains a typical, vertical organization. People continue to look up to their bosses instead of out to customers. Their loyalty is still to the functional fiefdoms in which they work, rather than to the overall company and its goals."

"Exactly," Laura replied emphatically, thinking of her own company.

Billy continued, "When people are empowered they don't look up the hierarchy for answers; they take responsibility to solve problems where they occur."

"How did your people respond to this new responsibility?" wondered Laura.

"At first, when people began to realize that they had more responsibility, many of them acted like they didn't want it. There were feelings left over from the old days when the attitude was 'That's not my job.' I remember hearing people say, 'If we're gonna be bosses, we should be getting more pay.' Handling this resistance to change was one of the functions of training which was critical to our efforts."

"What was the first thing you did to help change attitudes?" Laura asked.

"The Empowering Manager kept preaching the belief that decisions had to be made at the lowest level of the organization."

"Don't you mean 'at the highest level of the organization'?"

"Good catch," laughed Billy. "For front-line managers to do that, people were going to need new skills and different ways to operate. In short, they had to learn to act in responsible, decision-making teams."

"How did people take that?"

"They were confused. On the one hand it sounded good, but they didn't know what it meant. Neither did the managers. Everyone became discouraged and confused about what to do next, because they had never done this before either. It was a very frustrating period of time for everyone. It became clear you could not just announce empowerment and expect it to magically occur."

"That's what I've done," said Laura reflecting on the recent happenings at her company. "How did you pull out of this mess? Before I came to see the Empowering Manager and all of you, I was ready to throw in the towel and give up."

"We almost gave up ourselves," said Billy. "But then two things happened. First of all, the Empowering Manager didn't give up. He just persisted and kept talking to us as if we were all managers. A simple example is the *asking memo* he began to use."

"An asking memo?"

"You know how it goes in the typical unempowered organization: A memo comes down from on high saying we all need to start to save electricity or paper or some darn thing and people stand around and look at each other, smile and say, 'R-i-i-i-ght.' Then the manager comes out of his or her office and starts giving out orders about how it's to be done. Everybody feels like a naughty kid getting a lecture."

"That sounds like what I've seen all my life," sighed Laura.

"That's a *telling memo*," nodded Billy. "An *asking memo* is different. Take the case of the problem of saving resources. The Empowering Manager's memo would start out with the pertinent cost information, broken down to include your department's portion of the problem. The language of the memo would be short and sweet—no pep talk like, 'Let's all get behind this effort, etc.' It would be written simply, as if the readers needed this information so they could make decisions about it. When people in our department received one of those early asking memos from the Empowering Manager, they looked at each other, and then read the memo again..It was obvious that a departmental decision had to be made."

"It was just as obvious that no one was going to make it for us," Billy continued. "Pretty soon a dialogue would start. People would suggest things they could do. Then they'd decide what they *would* do."

"Early version of a team meeting," Laura put in. "How about carrying out the decision?"

"A snap," replied Billy. "Since the group had dealt with the problem on its own, the group 'owned' the solution. You know the way it is whenever you have a joint agreement with somebody. You both feel willing to carry it out, and also to tell the other person if they goof."

Laura nodded. "But I'm wondering about something. As you were developing these self-directed teams, what was the function of the managers?"

"That leads into the second thing that helped pull us through a period of high dissatisfaction and discouragement. Training! Managers knew they should be behaving differently and so did their team members, but nobody had a clue what to do until the Empowering Manager required us all to go to training."

"Required you to go to training?" echoed Laura.

"Yes," said Billy. "The Empowering Manager sees training not as an option, but as a value. He made training a requirement for everybody. He said that once you're scheduled for training you cannot be canceled out for any reason other than for a personal emergency. He said if we were ever tempted to pull someone from training we should call him and he'd work the person's shift."

Billy excused himself for a moment to respond to a question from a teammate.

"Required training?" wondered Laura. She was thinking about how training had worked in her own organization and others she'd seen. People were scheduled for training, then were pulled out by the supervisor because of some bureaucratic crisis—the vice president was making a visit, or more people were needed to take inventory. The Empowering Manager was obviously a leader committed to training as a way to bring needed change.

When Billy returned, Laura asked him how many calls the Empowering Manager got to work people's shifts.

"Not one," Billy answered. "When top managers are squarely behind the training of teams, it really smoothes the way. Remember, the second step to empowerment?"

"Clear boundaries lead to empowerment," said Laura. "I see. But I was wondering about all the dissatisfaction and discouragement you said people were experiencing. How did they work through it?"

"It took a while," said Melvin. "In our training we learned that groups, like individuals, go through predictable stages of development. They need different kinds of leadership at each stage."

"I'd like to hear more about the group stages," Laura said, once again getting out her notebook and pen.

"When a group first forms, members are typically enthusiastic, but they don't know how they're going to operate or who's going to play what role. That's called the *orientation* stage, and it's a time when a team needs strong, clear leadership. Someone has to set the agendas and organize the team's efforts."

"We didn't do that initially and our teams quickly moved into the second stage of development, the *dissatisfaction* stage. The reality of working as a team always seems to be more difficult than team members expect. In the training sessions we learned that teams in dissatisfaction need continued strong, clear leadership. But they also need support—someone to listen to their concerns and cheerlead for any progress made. We learned that, while this dissatisfaction stage is uncomfortable, it's a critical stage for ultimately becoming a high-performing team. It was in this dissatisfaction stage that we began to experiment with a role we still use today called the 'team coordinator.'"

Laura said, "We use team leaders in my company, but I have an idea you mean something a little different."

Billy nodded and said, "During the initial stages of our teams, the team coordinator, in many ways, acts like a manager. After a team moves into *resolution*—the third stage of team development, when members begin to learn to work together—we start to rotate the role of team coordinator among team members. The role of the coordinator is to support and facilitate the team."

"Also, it's important that team members understand what's going on in other areas," continued Billy, "So the coordinator attends weekly meetings of other departments and reports back to the team. This supports one of the organization's key values—cross training and cross utilization. Most of the decisions are made as a team, but the coordinator does the detail part, handling most of the paper work, scheduling people for vacation time, and so forth."

"The coordinator also trains the next person in rotation. We found that the team coordinator role becomes less critical as the final *production* stage of development is reached. A self-directed team acts to direct and support individual efforts itself. Again and again we learned the value of diversity as a real asset for dealing with the complex problems we face today. And when I talk about diversity I'm not just talking about race and sex, but also cultural background, as well as ability and opinion. We found that by drawing upon the unique skills, perspectives and knowledge of our team members, we developed far better solutions to our problems."

"So, as people's capabilities and contributions increase, the whole becomes greater than the sum of its parts," Laura summarized. "But I know that dealing with diversity can be difficult. It's much easier if everyone thinks alike. Haven't there ever been times when your teams just blew it?"

"Oh, sure," replied Billy. "Many times teams have learned the hard way. They've failed to utilize their resources and explore differences of opinion and tried to railroad decisions through."

"What happened?"

"It backfired. Next time the team had to decide something, those members whose ideas were ignored were uncooperative."

"So team development really involves using a lot of human relations skills."

"Absolutely. Any time we're to make a decision on a complex matter, we have to make sure every person has an opportunity to express his or her opinions and concerns. Not just to be fair, but so that each individual's talents can be brought to bear on the problem."

"When a team has reached the *production* stage, what is it able to do?" asked Laura.

"Over the last year or so, our teams have taken on more and more important decisions. A number of teams are now at a point where they actually do all or many of the functions traditionally viewed as the job of management—such as hiring and disciplining, performance evaluations, allocation of resources, quality assurance. These teams have really replaced the old management hierarchy."

"Amazing!" exclaimed Laura. She shook her head thoughtfully.

"What's wrong?" asked Billy.

"Several times today I've been faced with the evidence that empowerment really *works*, but it challenges my old beliefs."

"Hey, join the group," laughed Billy. "Most managers would say that if you trust people to be responsible for performing these functions and monitoring themselves, you're just asking for trouble. Maybe that would have been true of individuals the way they were accustomed to being treated under the old command-and-control management model. But when you empower people with information and boundaries and then train them to operate in self-directed teams, it's different. Since we started our journey to empowerment, I've come to see that people are an untapped resource. When they understand that you're trusting them to use their brains and their abilities, their own sense of responsibility comes to the fore. It's as if they've just been waiting for a chance to view the organization as their own, so they could improve it. Combine this intelligence and energy with a shared commitment to serving the customer and you've got something really powerful!"

"And what's more," continued Billy, "we continue to get better and better, and people continue to grow and develop new skills and abilities."

"In fact, if people are not continuing to grow and develop, then we find that they just don't seem to fit here anymore and they wind up leaving. As long as people want to continue to grow, continue to develop and continue to stretch themselves, they have a place here—they really fit. And that means we wind up having an organization that is profitable in many ways. I've developed a list of all the benefits of self-directed teams."

Benefits of Self-Directed Teams

- **Increased job satisfaction**

- **Attitude change from "have to" to "want to"**

- **Greater employee commitment**

- **Better communication between employees and management**

- **More efficient decision-making process**

- **Improved quality**

- **Reduced operating costs**

- **More profitable organization**

"And for all those pay-offs to occur," replied Laura, "your self-directed teams need to have a great deal of information. Now I understand further why information sharing was the first key to empowerment."

"You're absolutely right. And the need for information sharing continues to grow," explained Billy. "We have had to develop better mechanisms for recording information and for making it available to more people. One of the beauties of the new computer technology is that it allows us to put information into a form that's readily available to everyone through our PC networks. Everybody knows what's going on all the time. You see, for teams to be responsible, they demand a tremendous amount of information, more than they've ever had."

"We've also found as we've operated," Billy said, "that our team members are asking for only information that's really useful to them. That keeps us from being inundated with requests for information that they'll never use."

"That means we don't have to prepare as many reports as before," continued Billy, "but the reports we do prepare convey important information to our teams. Since teams are thinking about the importance of what they do, they're continually looking for better ways to do things and more ways to utilize the skills and abilities they have. After all, this is their organization, isn't it?"

"Fascinating," said Laura. "I think I'm finally getting a handle on how empowerment works and the impact it can have on organizational performance."

"Great! I'm glad I could help," smiled Billy.

Laura thanked Billy and headed out, thinking, "I'll stop by the Empowering Manager's office and see if he has any final pearls of wisdom before I start—I mean, restart—my journey to the Land of Empowerment."

As Laura walked back to the Empowering Manager's office she was feeling good about all she had learned.

"Well, are you ready to go?" smiled the Empowering Manager as he greeted her.

"I think so. Your associates have been very helpful. I've learned a great deal about empowerment. Implementing the three keys sounds like a real challenge, but also a great gift to everyone in our company."

"There is no doubt that you will need persistence in your belief that empowerment will work."

"Particularly with the last key—replacing the old hierarchy with self-directed teams," said Laura.

"That's always the part that makes managers have doubts about the whole process," said the Empowering Manager.

"When that confusion and dissatisfaction stage sets in, it must feel so out of control," Laura explained in a pained tone.

"Yes! Know why?" asked the Empowering Manager. "Because if you are going to be held accountable, you want to be in control."

"Right!"

"But the reality is that if you're going to empower people, you have to give up control and still remain accountable."

"That can be scary for a manager."

"Very. Especially when the organization gets to this stage of confusion and lack of leadership regarding next steps."

"The training sounds like it really helps," said Laura. "Just knowing that dissatisfaction is a natural, predictable stage of group development probably puts things in perspective."

"That's why I required the training," said the Empowering Manager. "I had tried before to empower people but didn't know the inevitability or severity of the dissatisfaction stage. When confusion and disillusionment began to occur, I was as scared as anyone. I was afraid I'd created a monster that none of us would be able to control. I wanted to head for the hills and abdicate."

"Did you?"

"No, but I've seen a lot of managers do just that, and empowerment often goes by the wayside."

"How did you hang in there?"

"Naive enthusiasm, probably," laughed the Empowering Manager. "I kept reminding myself and everyone else that people really did want to be empowered and it could make a performance difference in our organization. But I want to tell you, many a night I sat at my desk staring into space and wondering what I had gotten myself into. The Land of Empowerment seemed far away, over some distant mountain. I felt a strong sense of a leadership vacuum in the organization. Here I was asking people to make a major change in their way of relating to each other but neither I nor the other managers knew what guidance to provide. It was a very frustrating period for everyone."

"What happened?" quizzed Laura, now almost sitting on the edge of her seat.

"Gradually something interesting began to happen. It's like in the movies when the hero is on his last legs and you can't figure out how he's going to make it."

"But he always does!"

"Sure. That's what makes a good movie. The solution comes from some source you hadn't expected. That's what happened in our empowerment experience."

"Right in the midst of the leadership vacuum, flickering lights of empowerment began to shine from colleagues on the teams. Teams began to make important action decisions, individuals took the risk to speak out with suggestions and managers acted like facilitators."

"Out of the discomfort of the leadership vacuum, the very empowerment we wanted was born. The information sharing, new boundaries and skills training for teams began to pay off."

"Wow! I don't know if I could have hung in there," reflected Laura.

"That's why it's important to understand that the empowerment journey begins with direction during the orientation stage and requires you to add support to your efforts as natural dissatisfaction sets in. Any wavering from the vision at that time could be disastrous."

"So staying in the middle of the fray can speed up the movement to self-directed teams, even when you are unsure what to do to help?"

"That's it," said the Empowering Manager. "When it seems no one has the answer, people come forward in ways that can astonish you. And you can naturally become a facilitator who eventually becomes a group member."

"The key seems to be to stick to your beliefs," said Laura as she wrote some thoughts in her notebook.

"That's the only way your beliefs can become reality, but sometimes it can be very scary."

"Well, you said in the beginning that the journey to the Land of Empowerment would not be easy," said Laura. "I understand that thoroughly now, but I'm still ready to go."

"Good luck," said the Empowering Manager as they walked to the door.

"I'll need it," said Laura. "And you'll be hearing from me."

"Any time," replied the Empowering Manager as he waved good-bye to her. "I wish you persistence in your belief that empowerment will work."

Laura spent that evening collecting her thoughts and preparing to begin the empowerment journey with her organization.

She spent a good deal of time arranging and rearranging a set of cards on which she had transferred all her notes.

Finally, she came up with something she called the "Empowerment Game Plan." She decided she would give copies to everyone in her organization. It looked like this:

THE EMPOWERMENT GAME PLAN

Start with—

Sharing Information with Everyone

- Share performance information about the company; help people understand the business.
- Build trust through sharing.
- Set up self-monitoring possibilities.
- View mistakes as learning opportunities.
- Break down hierarchical thinking; help people behave as owners.

Then

Create Autonomy through Boundaries

- Clarify the big and little pictures.

- Clarify goals and roles.

- Define values and rules that underlie actions.

- Create rules and procedures that support empowerment.

- Provide needed training.

- Hold people accountable for results.

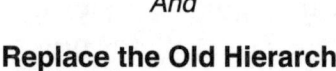

And

Replace the Old Hierarchy with Self-Directed Teams

- Provide direction and skills training for empowered teams.

- Provide support and encouragement for change.

- Use diversity as a team asset.

- Gradually give control to the teams.

- Recognize there will be some tough times.

Over the next few months, Laura and her company traveled along their own unique journey toward the Land of Empowerment. She made periodic calls at first to the Empowering Manager for advice and feedback. Very quickly, however, she and her associates became engaged in their own process of developing an empowered organization.

Over time, they became an empowered organization. Just as the Empowering Manager had acted as a guide for Laura, she found herself counseling other executives who were moving through their own journey. Again and again she heard herself say:

"Empowerment isn't magic.

It consists of a few simple steps and a lot of persistence."

* * *

Acknowledgments

There are so many people to thank and acknowledge for the learnings that led to this book. Inevitably, we will leave out some people, but we will do our best to be as complete as possible. In order to cover as many bases as possible (without writing another book), we will offer "Thank You" to a special group of people who have been most helpful in the formulation of our ideas. We will also offer acknowledgments to a much wider list of people and companies from whom we have learned as they reacted to earlier drafts of our book. To all, we wish to express our sincerest appreciation. We know they will recognize their contributions throughout the book.

Thank You

to the following companies and people in them, who have been courageous in their pioneering efforts to empower people and organizations:

Ralph Stayer of Johnsonville Foods for showing us and many others the way to create real empowerment

George Clifton and many others in the East Bay Region of Pacific Gas and Electric Company

Tom Jackson, Mike Squilante, Jeff Beck and a host of others in the Bank Funding Group of Advanta Corporation

Thank You, continued

George Wilson and many others at Florida Power & Light, plus Jo Anne Pitera and Barbara Dabney, formerly at Florida Power & Light

Jeanne Gruner and the Performance Management Task Force at Household International

Ron Floto, Dennis Carter, Lewis Payne, the top management team and the many district and store managers at Kash & Karry Stores

David Liddle of Circle K Stores (U.K.)

Lanny Julian and the amazing Field Staff of Ambassador Cards

Jim Pantelidas, Ron McIntosh, Gordon Olitch and Wolfgang Greogry of Petro-Canada

Mary Andrulivitz, Jack Kemp and all the Business Unit leaders at Sheppard-Pratt Hospital

Steve Wachter and the managers and employees of General Electric Information Services

Irv Rule and Matthew Reimann of Seimens Medical Systems, plus John Donnelly, formerly of Siemens Medical Systems

Acknowledgments

to the following people who read earlier drafts of the book and shared openly of their experiences in giving us feedback on the book:

Charles J. Loew with Motorola University

Julie Seeherman with Venture Stores

Rick Miller with the Boys & Girls Club of Phoenix

Tom Walczykowski with the FBI

Arnie Cole with the U.S. Army

Al Price with the Mauna Kea Beach Hotel

Joe Raymond with the Georgia Academy for Children and Youth Professionals

Don J. Carlos and Bill Carlos, brothers emeritus

Al Schneider with the Federal Communications Commission

Mike Perry with the E. I. DuPont Company

Bruce Dalgleish with General Mills Restaurants

Lou Reymann with Shimadzu Scientific Instruments

Mike Gill with Americom Cellular

Mike Louden with Louden Associates

John Coleman with CSX Corporation

Barbara Balter with the Robert B. Balter Company

Joe Bode with Black & Decker Corporation

Acknowledgments, continued

We would like to express our sincere thanks to Valerie Hall, Eleanor Terndrup, Michele Jansen, Harry Paul and Dale Strack for producing this book in a most efficient manner and to Bob Nelson for his helpful feedback and editing.

In addition, we owe an intellectual debt to many of our colleagues at Blanchard Training and Development, but especially Eunice Parisi-Carew and Don Carew for sharing their knowledge about team development, Jesse Stoner and Drea Zigarmi for their thinking about creating a compelling vision, Pat Zigarmi for new insights on Situational Leadership® II, and Dev Ogle for sharing his knowledge of continuous improvement and strategic thinking.

And most importantly, we would like to thank our wives, Marjorie Blanchard, Lynne Carlos and Ruth Anne Randolph whose support and challenging questions helped us refine this book to a high level of value for our readers.

Ken Blanchard would also like to acknowledge the impact on his thinking about self-directed teams from a visit with C. O. Woody, Rita Craig and some of the good folks from the Power Generation Business Unit of Florida Power & Light Company (FPL). In particular, a big One Minute Praising goes to Rick Beil, Eddie Childs, Mary Polk and Debra Shultz-Robinson who have been involved in self-directed teams at the Turkey Point Fossil and Cutler Plants. Their experience has been heartwarming and successful.

Acknowledgments, continued

John Carlos would also like to praise:

Mike Vance...my phantom mentor for over 20 years

Rick and Ester Miller...for standing by me when many didn't

Lino and Kelly Antunes, Andee and Todd Oleno...my children who have always been an inspiration

Gordon Dolan...a good friend and colleague

1st Sgt. Harold J. Merton...who first taught me about leadership

Alan Randolph would also like to praise:

Barry Posner and Jackie Schmidt-Posner for their constant friendship and colleagueship

Father Vincent Dwyer for his early inspiration

Ashley, Shannon and Liza, my children who inspire me to be empowered and to empower them

Dean Dan Costello of the Merrick School of Business, University of Baltimore for taking on the challenge to empower a business school

About the Authors

Ken Blanchard has had tremendous impact on the day-to-day management of people and companies.

As a writer in the field of management, his impact has been far reaching. His One Minute Manager Library, which includes *The One Minute Manager*® (1982), *Putting the One Minute Manager to Work* (1984), *Leadership and the One Minute Manager* (1985), *The One Minute Manager Gets Fit* (1986), *The One Minute Manager Meets the Monkey* (1989), and *The One Minute Manager Builds High-Performing Teams* (1990), has collectively sold more than seven million copies and has been translated into more than twenty languages.

He is also co-author with Dr. Paul Hersey of *Management of Organizational Behavior,* a classic textbook now in its sixth edition, *The Power of Ethical Management* with Dr. Norman Vincent Peale, and *Raving Fans: A Revolutionary Approach to Customer Service* with Sheldon Bowles. His most recent book, *We Are the Beloved* highlights his spiritual journey.

Ken is chairman of Blanchard Training and Development, Inc., a full-service management consulting and training company, which he founded in 1979 with his wife, Marjorie. He maintains a visiting lectureship at Cornell University, where he also serves as Trustee Emeritus. The Blanchards live in San Diego.

About the Authors, continued

John P. Carlos is a highly skilled management consultant, trainer, and motivational speaker.

With 25 years of hands-on experience as a manager and trainer, his knowledge of organizational and management development, succession planning, team empowerment, customer service, leadership training, and managing diversity is considered to be at the leading edge of today's technology. John specializes in organization and people development, empowering teams, and developing companies to deliver legendary customer service.

As a speaker, he is best known for his humorous and insightful real-life stories and his ability to get people to focus on their own behavior. His years of experience include both private, for profit and non-profit organizations, and range from convenience stores, to hotels and resorts, to residential treatment schools for adjudicated, hard-to-place teenagers. For ten years he was the director of training for Circle K, a retail food company with over 5,000 outlets worldwide. He heads his own consulting group and is a senior associate with Blanchard Training and Development, Inc.

John received a bachelor's degree in business and an M.B.A. from Columbia Pacific University. He now lives with his wife Lynne in Phoenix, Arizona. His two grown daughters, Kelly and Andee and his sons-in-law, Todd and Lino also live in Arizona.

About the Authors, continued

Alan Randolph is an internationally respected and highly accomplished management educator and consultant.

Alan has consulted on management and organization, with domestic and international organizations in both public and private sectors. His specialties include empowerment, project planning and management, performance management, leadership, customer service and team building. As a seminar presenter and speaker, he is comfortable, clear and to the point.

Alan is professor of management and director of leadership and international programs at the University of Baltimore's Merrick School of Business and a senior associate with Blanchard Training and Development, Inc. (BTD). He has published a variety of articles in both practitioner and academic journals. He is co-author with Barry Posner of *Getting the Job Done: Managing Project Teams and Task Forces for Success* (1992) and with Robert Miles and Edward Kemery of *The Organization Game* (1993).

Alan holds a bachelor's degree in industrial engineering from Georgia Institute of Technology, a master's degree in personnel and industrial relations, and a Ph.D. in business administration from the University of Massachusetts, Amherst.

He and his wife Ruth Anne, also a senior associate with BTD, and their daughters, Ashley, Shannon and Liza, live in Baltimore, Maryland.

Services Available

Blanchard Training and Development, Inc., (BTD) is a full-service consulting and training company in the areas of empowerment, leadership, teamwork, performance management, customer service, quality management, ethics and visioning.

Empowerment is the latest in a long line of key leadership concepts that BTD has made understandable and accessible to managers in both the private and public sectors. Based upon research and consultation with a wide variety of companies over the last eight years, the empowerment concepts have been developed to assist managers in guiding their people and organizations to the Land of Empowerment. The keys to empowerment make significant links to many other topics that have been developed by BTD including: Situational Leadership® II, Building High Performing Teams, Creating Your Organization's Future, Total Quality Leadership, Situational Self Leadership and Partnering for Performance Management.

BTD offers consulting, training, and speaking services, as well as a complete product line of videos and print material designed to enhance individual and organizational learning and change.

Services Available, continued

To learn more about how BTD can help empower your people and organization please call or write:

Blanchard Training and Development, Inc.
125 State Place
Escondido, CA 92029
800-728-6000 or 619-489-5005

You may contact Ken Blanchard and John Carlos directly through the BTD office in Escondido at the above numbers. You may contact Alan Randolph directly at the BTD office in Baltimore at 410-321-8231.

The authors are also available "on-line" through PRODIGY at DMVT33A or CompuSERV at 76121,1545.

An Invitation...

In our quest for continued learning about empowerment and the journey to get there, we invite you to send us stories describing your experiences and insights about empowerment. You may send your comments to:

The Empowerment File
Ken Blanchard, John Carlos and Alan Randolph
Blanchard Training and Development, Inc.
125 State Place
Escondido, CA 92029